"Every organization has a culture. It will either be by design or by default. *Remarkable!* will help leaders intentionally craft a compelling culture, where team members are inspired to bring their best to the table every single day."

—John Maxwell, *New York Times* bestselling author, speaker, and founder, the John Maxwell Co.

"I make my living by studying culture and then sharing insights and observations that make people laugh. But creating the culture of an organization is no laughing matter. People's lives and livelihoods are at stake. And yet, I think some of the same process applies. You must study the culture of your organization and then share insights and other observations that inspire and motivate people. This book is filled with such insights. If you study and apply them, well, then who knows, you might be Remarkable!"

—Jeff Foxworthy, author, actor, talk show host, comedian, and friend of rednecks everywhere

"Indeed, true transformation begins on the inside before it's revealed on the outside. This book is a catalyst for personal and cultural transformation."

—Orrin Woodward, *New York Times* bestselling author and founder, LIFE Leadership

"If fate has brought this book to your attention—you need to read it. My MBA professor once told me that the best professors don't just teach you—they teach you how to think. Reading *Remarkable!* makes you feel like you're a fly on the wall, listening to the most important conversation about life and business that you never heard."

—Rick Schirmer, founder and CEO, PartnersHub (former brand strategy executive, the Walt Disney Company)

"*Remarkable!* is about the powerful idea of organizing our businesses and our lives around the pursuit of values. It is not enough to know the 'what' and the 'how.' When we understand and embrace the 'why,' it changes everything."

—Dave Stockert, CEO, Post Properties

Nothing is so common-place as to wish to be remarkable.

OLIVER WENDELL HOLMES SR.,
THE AUTOCRAT OF THE BREAKFAST TABLE

REMARKABLE!

MAXIMIZING RESULTS
THROUGH VALUE CREATION

Dr. Randy Ross
and David Salyers

BakerBooks
a division of Baker Publishing Group
Grand Rapids, Michigan

© 2016 by Randy Ross and David Salyers

Published by Baker Books
a division of Baker Publishing Group
P.O. Box 6287, Grand Rapids, MI 49516-6287
www.bakerbooks.com

Printed in the United States of America

Library of Congress Cataloging-in-Publication Data is on file at the Library of Congress, Washington, DC

ISBN 978-0-8010-1883-1

The people and situations in this book are fictional. Any resemblance to actual events, locales, or persons, living or dead, is coincidental, with one notable exception. Robert S. Hartman, known to many as the father of modern axiology, was a well-known and highly respected philosopher, educator, scientist, and business consultant. For more information on Robert S. Hartman, please refer to the tribute in the appendix.

In keeping with biblical principles of creation stewardship, Baker Publishing Group advocates the responsible use of our natural resources. As a member of the Green Press Initiative, our company uses recycled paper when possible. The text paper of this book is composed in part of post-consumer waste.

16 17 18 19 20 21 22   7 6 5 4 3 2 1

Remarkable! is dedicated to the most Remarkable! people in our lives: LuAnne and Lynn for their unconditional love and support. And to Ryan, Lindsay, and Colton, as well as Amanda, Nick, and Daniel, whose futures we hope will be brightened by the application of these truths.

Contents

Contents

Foreword

I have always believed that a good name is more desirable than great riches. While profits are important in any business, maintaining a strong sense of values and living out your convictions are imperative. If a company's good name to the outside world is its brand, then its real character is revealed in its culture. And while there is much discussion about the need to create a compelling corporate culture in the marketplace today, very few understand the dynamics at play and how to address them effectively. Taking simple truths and placing them in a corporate parable, *Remarkable!* provides the reader with both an enjoyable format and transformational insights.

I am convinced that if you help others get what they want, then you will eventually get what you want. A deep love for people causes you to focus your efforts on providing the best for them rather than constantly thinking about what you want to receive from them. This simple concept transforms relationships and the work experience and is at the core of good business.

The truths contained within the pages of what you are about to read are a clear and succinct articulation of the principles that create a superior advantage in business. If embraced and applied, these principles can have a profoundly positive impact on the culture of any company. At the same time, they have the power to enhance your professional life. But please don't stop there. Apply them to your personal life and watch them transform your closest relationships as well. After all, there is no better way to invest your time and energy than in strengthening relationships. It truly is "my pleasure" to encourage you to read and apply the truths contained within the pages of *Remarkable!*

S. Truett Cathy

founder, Chick-fil-A, Inc.

Introduction

There are millions of businesses and organizations, but only a handful of them could be described as Remarkable! Have you ever wondered why? Remarkable means notably or conspicuously unusual, extraordinary, worthy of notice or attention. The ideas explored in this book have come from a lifetime of observing some extraordinary people and organizations as they live out their conspicuously unusual ideas, producing uncommon results. The effect is that those who work for and benefit from these people and organizations find themselves with an irrepressible desire to "remark about them." What is it that these people know that others seemingly do not? How does their view of the world lead them to think and behave differently than others? When faced with the same opportunities and challenges, how are their choices different . . . and why?

This book is an attempt to answer these questions and resolve the most important issue facing businesses today. Once you understand the basic premise and apply the principles contained within these pages, a transformation is almost certain. We encourage you to begin a revolution that will infuse new life and energy into your organization and help people find significance and fulfillment in their work.

Life is either limited or enhanced by your choices. Leadership is about influencing people to make conspicuously unusual choices that bring health and happiness to life and work. The choices you make will eventually make you. We challenge you to choose to be Remarkable!

—Dr. Randy Ross and David Salyers

. . . .

**We want to offer you an opportunity
to take the Remarkable Engagement Index.**

**For more details,
please see the back of the book.**

. . . .

PART 1

ASSESSMENT

Advertising is a tax you pay for being unremarkable.

ROBERT STEPHENS,
FOUNDER, GEEK SQUAD

1

Shifting Gears

The tires thumped in syncopated rhythm with the joints in the pavement of the overpass just north of the city. Dusty's mind was spinning as quickly as the wheels on his candy apple red 1968 Ford Thunderbird convertible, an innocent indulgence he had afforded himself shortly after his thirty-ninth birthday. The T-Bird was a midlife purchase that brought him much joy. It had rolled off the assembly line the very month of his birth, and he had always been drawn to its sheer power and sleek elegance. He took great pride in keeping it in mint condition and enjoyed the attention it garnered when he occasionally took it on road trips to the beach. Though he rarely drove the car to work, today he was glad he had. With the top down and the sun out, it was pure therapy. He actually welcomed this commute home because it gave him time to reflect on everything that had happened that week at work.

Dusty Harts was a senior vice president at Query, a customer care service provider in the utilities industry. Working from the corporate office in Atlanta, Dusty was responsible for the firm's three call centers in the southeast United States. With more than eight hundred energy advisors in his chain of command, the demands he faced as the leader of such a heavily customer-facing operation were formidable. To add to the burden, two weeks earlier he had received the results of Query's recent Employee Engagement Survey, and one could refer generously to the scores as "not good."

For two years, Dusty had taken comfort in the fact that employee turnover was at an all-time low. He was optimistic that somehow the company had finally slowed the spin of the revolving back door that had previously churned associates through the organization. Now, it appeared, the bubble had burst. Dusty knew that economic winds were adverse and few companies were hiring in the market. That had kept the issues hidden by limiting options for the disgruntled and disillusioned. Despite the fact that his teams were meeting client expectations, morale was a constant concern. His gut told him that things were not all good, but he'd never expected such an abrupt reality check. The survey painted a picture of unhappy, unmotivated teams, with a significant number of employees seemingly slogging through the drudgery of their daily activities. By their responses, many team members had indicated that they were experiencing little satisfaction or fulfillment. The findings from the survey had sent leaders throughout the organization into a tailspin.

Employee engagement had become a critical metric for Query ever since Gallup published studies definitively linking higher levels of engagement to higher productivity. Leaders intuitively knew that the employee experience and the customer experience were inseparably linked, but this research actually quantified the connection. If employees were unhappy in their roles and brought little enthusiasm to the job, then that lackluster attitude would most certainly carry over into their encounters with customers.

But it had also been firmly established that the higher the emotional attachment to one's work, the more passionate and productive the performance. Measuring, monitoring, and moving engagement levels in a positive direction could produce profound results. Therefore, engagement was at the heart of what Query called its *transformational triad*. This three-pronged mission statement encapsulated their commitment to engagement. It simply read: "Engage, empower, and enrich the life of every colleague and customer." It sounded impressive, and it was certainly visible. It was displayed prominently in the lobby alongside the vision and values statements, as well as on plaques and posters throughout the building. The real challenge was in figuring out how to add some walk to the talk. Dusty often wondered how many of his team members could even explain these statements, much less embody them.

Once the survey results had reached the leadership team, Jim Mitchell, the chief financial officer, had formed a task force to address the troublesome findings. The ad hoc team's stated objective was to determine a course of action that would turn the tide and reverse the downward trend. Dusty had been tapped to be a part of the task force, and he wanted to believe that Jim placed great confidence in his judgment and valued him as a key player in the transformation process. After all, Jim had been influential in hiring Dusty six years ago. Since that time, Jim had served as a confidant and mentor. He was one of Dusty's biggest cheerleaders.

However, Dusty's team members were among those who rated their work experience poorly on the survey. He wondered if his reputation as a leader had been tarnished by the less-than-stellar report and worried that it would be taken as a reflection of his leadership. Either way, it threw him into the proverbial lion's den, staring into the teeth of what was sure to be a difficult season as the task force tried to determine what was causing their corporate sails to luff in the wind.

Dusty was trying not to let the whirlwind in his head prevent him from enjoying the beginning of a beautiful spring weekend. Pushing his concerns to the back of his mind, he approached the exit that would take him to his well-manicured community in the suburbs of north Atlanta.

As he approached a turn and depressed the clutch, he struggled to get the car into a lower gear. He had experienced difficulties in shifting the last few times he had driven his "ball of fire," as he affectionately called it. This time the grinding was unnerving. It was time to have someone look at what might be malfunctioning, and he knew just where to take the car. He decided to run by Classic Car Care, where he had developed a good relationship with the owner. If he could get there by six o'clock, someone might be able to take a look and get the work done the following day. That way, he reasoned, he could have the car back in time to drive it to church on Sunday morning, something he loved to do when the weather permitted.

Dusty pulled up to Classic Car Care right at six o'clock, fearing that he might have missed his window of opportunity. He fully expected that he would have to come back again the next morning. But true to form, Fred came sauntering out to greet him.

Fred Walters was the owner of Classic Car Care. He always made Dusty feel like they were best friends, even though the only time he ever saw Fred was when he brought the family vehicles in for routine maintenance. Fred was a stately man in his midsixties, with a tall frame and wavy gray hair. He was unusually fit for a man his age and always neatly dressed. Dusty often thought it odd that Fred's khaki pants and shirt were perfectly pressed, even if they sported oil and grime from the shop. Half the time Fred could be found out front with customers and the other half he would be working diligently on a car in one of the bays. He always seemed to be remarkably at ease, whether working with a wrench in his hand or on the phone with a customer.

"Hey, Dusty, what brings you our way on a beautiful day like today?" Fred asked with his usual unassuming smile.

By the warm greeting and light tone in his voice, you would have thought Fred had all the time in the world to talk with Dusty.

"I've been having difficulty shifting gears, and I was wondering if you could take a look and see what's going on. I think the clutch is going out," Dusty answered.

"We're closing for the night. If you'll pull her into the second bay, I'll give her a once-over first thing in the morning and give you a call. Does that work for you?" Fred asked.

"That would be great," Dusty responded. "I'll call my son and have him come pick me up."

"Don't bother. I can drop you off on my way home," Fred offered. "I'll still be able to get cleaned up in time to take Anne out for our date tonight. Come on."

Accepting Fred's offer, Dusty pulled the T-Bird into the bay while Fred gave a few last instructions to his partner in the front office. Then the two men climbed into Fred's restored vintage 1948 pickup and drove away, chatting about their love of classic cars like two giddy teenage girls talking about boys.

2

The Clutch

Dusty's cell phone rang shortly after nine o'clock the following morning. It was Fred calling.

"You were right," he said. "The clutch has gone out and needs to be replaced. I can get the parts and have it ready for you by the end of the day."

"Perfect," Dusty responded. "I'll swing by late this afternoon to pick it up."

Shortly after four o'clock, Dusty's seventeen-year-old son, Mike, dropped him off at Classic Car Care. His T-Bird was sitting in the parking lot, washed and ready to go. It was standard operating procedure at Classic to take all the cars next door to the car wash before returning them to their owners. It was a nice touch that clients appreciated.

Dusty walked into the waiting area. He could see Fred talking with someone in his office. When Fred saw Dusty, he motioned for him to take a seat. The day was winding down, and the only other person on the premises was a mechanic who was cleaning up the shop. Dusty sat down in one of the comfortable leather chairs and grabbed the current copy of *Harvard Business Review* off the coffee table. It struck him as a bit strange that Fred would be receiving *HBR* at the shop, but it was a fleeting thought. He quickly became engrossed in an article entitled "Managing Yourself: The Paradox of Excellence." He couldn't hear the conversation through the open doorway, but it was punctuated by laughter, which occasionally distracted him from his reading.

A while later, Fred walked out of his office and said, "Hey, Dusty, I want you to meet an old friend of mine. This is Howard Levine. Howard's been a friend since college when we used to compete for the attention of the same girls. He dropped by today in search of sage advice and business counsel," Fred quipped in a tongue-in-cheek sort of way.

"It's a pleasure to meet you, Dusty," said Howard. "Fred was showing me your car earlier. It's a beauty!" Dusty was a bit taken aback. He knew Howard Levine by reputation. One of the most widely respected business leaders in the southeastern United States, he had taken the helm of two Fortune 500 companies that were headed for the rocks and turned them around. Against significant odds, he had steered both companies clear of disaster, brought them through rough waters, and made them profitable again. Levine had been lauded by many as a master of business transformation.

"Thank you," Dusty stammered. "Fred helps me keep it in good running condition. It's a pleasure to meet you as well."

"Well, I'd better be on my way. I've mined what little knowledge Fred has left and taken the last nuggets of gold," Howard taunted.

"Don't pay any attention to him," Fred said. "He's still jealous that I married the only girl he couldn't get a date with during college. Her standards were much too high."

With that good-natured barb still in his side, Howard laughed and hugged Fred before disappearing out the door. "Come on into my office if you have the time," Fred offered.

"Sure," Dusty said. Though overwhelmed by the fact that he had just met Howard Levine, Dusty tried to remain composed. He had never been in Fred's office. It was modest but nicely appointed, with pictures of family and friends taken during trips and special occasions decorating most of the shelves and walls. Rather than sitting behind his desk, Fred gestured toward a table in the corner and offered Dusty a chair. While Dusty was taking his seat, Fred reached into the closet and retrieved two bottles of water from a small refrigerator. Dusty couldn't contain his curiosity any longer. As Fred handed him a bottle, he started blurting out questions.

"Did you really go to school with Howard Levine? Didn't he graduate from Harvard?"

"Dragged him through is more accurate." Fred laughed. "We were roommates for two years. I'm still not sure how either one of us made it through the MBA program. He was constantly distracted by living life large, and I was too serious for both of us."

"You graduated from Harvard Business School?"

"Surprised? I haven't always owned this shop. Tinkering with cars is a passion that I always wanted to turn into a business. I guess you could say I'm enjoying my retirement. I was lucky enough to figure out a way to get people to pay me to do what I love—working on cars. I like to fix things and get them running smoothly."

For a moment, Dusty sat in stunned silence. The guy who'd just fixed his car was a Harvard graduate and Howard Levine's former roommate. "So, he *really was* seeking business advice from you?"

"Not really," Fred said. "We miss the banter of the old days and enjoy popping in on one another now and then to kick around a few ideas. He swung by to wish me a happy anniversary. As of yesterday, Anne and I have been married for forty-two years. And yes, it is a fact that he never did get a date with her. But enough about me. I wanted to ask you about something that came up in our conversation last night as I was driving you home."

"Sure, what was that?"

"Actually, it wasn't so much what you said as it was what you didn't say. When I asked you how work was going, your answer seemed vague and evasive. Not quite the response I'd expect from someone who was enjoying his work," Fred answered.

His comment was pointed but not the least bit offensive. When Fred had asked about his work the night before, Dusty had taken the question as small talk. Now he realized that Fred was genuinely interested.

"Is everything all right at work?" Fred asked.

"To be honest," Dusty answered, "things at work are a bit tense. Life in a call center environment is hard enough. Now, based on a company-wide survey, our engagement scores are at an all-time low, and everyone is in a panic to figure out what's wrong and how to turn things around. Just when I thought things were sailing along smoothly, I get hit by this squall!"

"I could tell something was bothering you," Fred said. "Let me ask you something. What made you think things were going smoothly?"

"Well, our attrition rates have been good, and we've been hitting our numbers."

"But now, through the survey, people are telling you that they aren't happy with their current work situation. And low engagement could mean lost opportunities, lackluster customer support, and a significant number of people who have already emotionally disengaged and are only staying for a paycheck."

Dusty wasn't sure if that was a question or an observation. Either way, it was astute.

"Sounds to me like you are having a problem with your clutch," Fred suggested.

Now Dusty was really confused. He wondered why Fred was changing the subject back to his car.

"I thought you said that you fixed the clutch?"

"I did—on your T-Bird. But I'm referring to your work. The clutch, as you well know, provides the linkage between the engine and the transmission, which ultimately provides power to the drive shaft. When the clutch is engaged, the power produced by the engine is harnessed and transferred to the drive shaft to produce motion. If the clutch is disengaged, then the engine continues to produce power, but it's uncoupled from the drive shaft, rendering it incapable of turning the wheels and garnering traction. You literally cannot 'get things into gear' when the clutch is malfunctioning. As I said, you have a clutch problem—at work!

"The condition of the clutch determines how much discretionary effort your people are willing to put forth. It reflects the level of loyalty, passion, and enthusiasm your team members bring to the endeavor. In the final analysis, the clutch will determine momentum and levels of performance."

What a great analogy of engagement, Dusty thought. He wanted to understand more fully what Fred meant. So he asked him a clarifying question.

"What exactly do you mean by 'the clutch'?"

"The clutch," Fred said, "is the mechanism that provides for the engagement of two or more components to produce motion. On an interpersonal level, a clutch situation is any encounter that requires the engagement of two or more people to create progress—which is just about every human interaction. A clutch situation could be a challenge, a setback, a new directive, or a vast opportunity that calls your team to step it up. It could be anything that rocks the status quo, or it could be something as simple as a conversation between colleagues. Any situation that requires two or more parties to work together is a clutch situation.

> *A clutch situation is any encounter that requires the engagement of two or more people to create progress.*

"As you know, 'clutch player' is a term often used in sports. It refers to a player who—in the heat of the moment, when the pressure is high—responds with stellar performance. A clutch player has the emotional constitution of a winner. Clutch players become evident in times of challenge and transition. In the clutch, a person will either step up to the plate or withdraw to the safety of the shadows. When the game is on the line, a clutch player always wants the ball! If you have an engagement problem, then you have a clutch problem."

"So what do I do about it?" asked Dusty.

"You fix it—just like I fixed the clutch on your T-Bird," Fred said matter-of-factly.

"All right, but how do I do that?" Dusty asked as he leaned forward in his chair.

"Now that's a conversation for another day," Fred responded. "Anne and I have some more celebrating to do this weekend, and it's time for me to get home. But, if you have any interest, I'd be happy to continue the conversation another time." With that offer hanging in the air, Fred escorted Dusty to the waiting area, where he gave him his paperwork and keys before ushering him to the front door.

"Enjoy the rest of your weekend," Fred said to Dusty.

Almost as quickly as he could say, "Thanks, you too," Dusty found himself standing outside of Classic Car Care. He wasn't sure what had just happened. He felt like a quarterback who had just been blindsided in the pocket. He had come to pick up his car and was floored by insights about his business—offered up by his mechanic—who had an MBA from Harvard!

After driving home, Dusty went straight to his computer and googled Fred Walters. What he discovered was impressive. Eight years earlier, Fred had been the CEO of Performax, a thriving multinational software company. One of the industry's leading trade magazines had listed Performax as one of the *Best Places to Work* the last five years Fred led the company. The *Business Chronicle* had also recognized the company as a leader in cultural transformation. Dusty couldn't believe what he was reading. And he couldn't wait to call Classic Car Care again on Monday to schedule an oil change for his wife's car—whether or not it needed it.

3

Tune-Up

Dusty was in the office early Monday morning to prepare for meetings that started at eight o'clock. Shortly after ten thirty, he was back at his desk dialing Classic Car Care.

"May I speak with Fred, please? This is Dusty Harts."

"He's not here today, Mr. Harts. He usually comes in on Tuesdays, Thursdays, and Fridays. May I help you?"

"I want to schedule a time for an oil change," Dusty said.

"I can help you with that. When would you like to come in?"

"Whenever Fred is around and you're not too busy," Dusty blurted out before he realized how silly it sounded. "What I mean is, well, I would really like to spend some time talking with Fred, if that's possible, while the oil is being changed," Dusty stammered. "When would you suggest I come in?"

"Actually, you aren't the first person to ask that question. Right now, it looks like he might have some time on Thursday afternoon. Why don't you come in around four o'clock, and I'll ask him to hold the hour for you. Does that work?"

"That would be great. Thanks so much. I'll see you Thursday at four o'clock," Dusty confirmed.

The rest of the day was a blur. After clearing his calendar after three o'clock on Thursday afternoon, he went straight into two phone conferences, a lunch meeting with his team leaders that ran until midafternoon, and then a meeting with members of the IT team to troubleshoot a technical problem. By late afternoon, he was back at his desk ready to prep for his meeting the next morning with the Employee Engagement Task Force.

Dusty retrieved a copy of the latest Employee Engagement Survey report and gathered all of the research and notes he had compiled over the years that might be relevant. He reviewed the reports from the previous two surveys and was painfully reminded of the obvious downward trending. He then perused his notes from the focus groups and the list of action items the leadership team had crafted to address the areas that "needed development." And last but not least, he examined the implementation notes on the fulfillment of each corrective initiative across the organization.

After dissecting the reports for more than an hour, Dusty was growing frustrated. He began to question why the multiple corporate initiatives had garnered such meager results. In some instances, they had absolutely no positive impact whatsoever. It just didn't make sense. It seemed illogical to have spent the time, energy, and resources necessary to create massive initiatives only to fail in moving the needle of engagement northward. Dusty couldn't help but wonder why their corporate compass was so badly broken.

Dusty had spearheaded two of those initiatives. One of them was still a source of deep frustration for him. It addressed educational opportunities—or the supposed lack thereof—within the company. One of the areas in which the scores had been comparatively low was in regard to whether or not there were "sufficient opportunities for team members to learn and grow." In the subsequent focus groups, it became obvious that employees were not asking for more job-related developmental opportunities. Instead, associates wanted the opportunity to grow in life-management skills—the "soft stuff," as Dusty often called it. Specific topics suggested were related to effectively dealing with personal finances, work-life balance, and conflict management. In response, every quarter the company offered a series of workshops presented by highly qualified and highly paid professionals. Attendance was purely voluntary. After nine months, the workshops were canceled due to lack of attendance.

What really never made much sense to Dusty was why the company would be expected to fill a void that should have been addressed in the home or in school. If someone was having trouble managing their finances, should the company really be expected to help them develop a personal budget? Beyond that, some of the questions on the survey related to aspects of individual socialization that Dusty was certain the organization could do little about. One particular question that consistently came up really got under Dusty's skin: "Do you have a best friend at work?" He thought the question itself was strange. He understood that working in an environment in which you consider some of your colleagues to be your friends is good for morale. But what if someone doesn't have a BFF at work? Is it the manager's responsibility to appoint a best friend to every employee? The thought made Dusty chuckle and helped to break the tension he was feeling, if only momentarily.

He mused over the fact that so many team leaders had become frustrated that, despite a lack of clarity, they were tasked with identifying corrective measures. Not surprisingly, the "remedies" often quickly degenerated into nothing more than feeble attempts to boost morale by organizing bowling outings and pizza parties. There was a growing knot in the pit of Dusty's stomach as he thought about the impending task force meeting. He wasn't looking forward to it.

The next morning, Dusty arrived at the conference room a few minutes early and was greeted by Jim Mitchell. Jim had always been a big champion of employee engagement. As the CFO, he was absolutely convinced by the research that high levels of engagement are directly linked to high levels of productivity. Though Dusty shared the same conviction with a little less passion, he highly respected Jim and his opinion. He had been a source of invaluable feedback at crucial times when Dusty needed objective counsel.

Dusty knew Jim to be insightful, straight-shooting, and fair. In short, he trusted his leadership. Many times Dusty had heard Jim say, "Where trust is high, resistance is low. Therefore, change and progress come quickly. Conversely, where trust is low, resistance is high. Therefore, change and progress come slowly." Through Jim's influence, Dusty had grown to understand the importance of building high-trust relationships.

"Good morning, Dusty," Jim said with a smile. "Thanks for agreeing to be a part of the task force again. I'm looking forward to getting your seasoned insights on how you think we can get some traction around engagement."

The word *traction* triggered a brief flashback to Dusty's conversation with Fred Walters about the clutch.

"Happy to be invited," Dusty said reflexively, though it was a bit disingenuous.

Dusty wanted to ask Jim a few questions that had been churning in his head. Before he could get the words out, other team members began to fill the room. He decided to wait until he could catch Jim privately.

Where trust is high, resistance is low. Therefore, change and progress come quickly. Conversely, where trust is low, resistance is high. Therefore, change and progress come slowly.

The meeting was basically what Dusty had expected. It began with a review of the report, highlighting the "opportunities for improvement." Then the group spent time comparing scores with those of other leading organizations in the industry. This, of course, was followed by some lively discussion about which areas could potentially provide a lift to sagging employee morale. It was déjà vu for Dusty. This ride was all too familiar. He wanted to get off this emotional Ferris wheel, which was moving round and round but going nowhere. He knew exactly what was coming next—the assignment to go back and conduct focus groups to get additional feedback that could be thrown into the meat grinder. He was about to interject with an objection, without any thought given to offering a solution, when the meeting took an unexpected turn.

Jim stood up for the first time during the meeting. Up to that point, he had primarily listened. As a veteran facilitator, he was a master at asking catalytic questions. But now it was time for him to speak. His face and tone conveyed his intensity. He had everyone's undivided attention.

"If our company were a car, I would say we are long overdue for a tune-up or possibly an engine overhaul. If we want to run smoothly and efficiently, it's time to do a multipoint checkup. Given all that we've discussed today, there are a few questions I want you to ponder. Since our efforts in the past have failed to achieve the desired results, how can we do things differently this time around? Albert Einstein once said, 'Problems cannot be solved by the same level of thinking that created them.' We need to look at engagement through a whole new lens.

"We're going to meet again in a week. In the meantime, I want you to give this your highest level of thinking. We have the collective intelligence to provide some clarity for our organization. I don't want you to look at what our competitors are doing. Excellence never comes by comparing yourself to others. If by comparison we think we are better than others, then pride sets in and we may gloat. If we fall short in our comparison to others, then we may struggle with morale issues and a sense of inferiority, which can negatively impact performance.

"I want us to own our destiny and dream a dream that will inspire everyone to bring their best to the table each and every day. I want us to reach our full potential as individuals and as a company."

Jim projected a slide onto the screen that read:

A Compelling Culture Is Created When People:

- BELIEVE the best IN one another
- WANT the best FOR one another
- EXPECT the best FROM one another

Then he continued by saying, "I want us to craft a culture in which we believe the very best *in* our people, provide the very best *for* our people, and call out the very best *from* our people. As leaders, we know exactly what we want from our people. But what do we want for our people? Do we have a culture of high trust that believes the best in our people while we seek the best for our people? What would that look like, and what is it going to take to get us there? When we answer these questions, we will be moving in the right direction. How do we chart a course with such a heading?"

With Jim's questions wafting in the air, the meeting was adjourned. Dusty sat motionless for a moment. Jim had presented him with a challenge before he could utter his objection. Nonetheless, he liked it. The challenge actually gave him hope that things might be different this time around. He could hardly wait for his oil change appointment.

4

The Oil Change

Dusty finally remembered late Wednesday night to tell his wife, Lisa, that he was going to get the oil changed in her car the following afternoon. She reminded him that it had been changed recently and wasn't due for another thousand miles. Dusty was sure this was the only time in their entire marriage that she had actually remembered when the oil had been changed! So Dusty explained that he was really trying to get some personal time with Fred Walters to discuss a few business matters.

"Then why didn't you just ask him to meet you for coffee instead of changing the oil when it's not needed?" Lisa asked.

Dusty wondered why her memory was serving her so well all of a sudden. And since when had she become so logical? "Would you care to drive the T-Bird while I have your car?" he asked.

"No, I'm good. I know that's your baby. I have plenty of catching up to do around the house tomorrow."

Good deal, Dusty mused.

As he drove to the office the following morning, Dusty wondered why he'd been hesitant to simply tell Lisa the truth about the oil change. Their relationship had certainly seen better days. Over the course of their nineteen-year marriage, they had drifted apart. Their busy schedules and different interests had caused them to spend time in separate spheres. It seemed like they passed each other only long enough to exchange necessary information. Dusty had always defined himself by his work, spending an inordinate amount of time at the office. He was proud of the reputation he had worked so hard to garner. For him, a strong work ethic meant being the first one in the office and the last one out. On Saturdays, he justified his morning round of golf at the club as his reward for having worked so hard during the week. While he loved golfing with his buddies, it left little time on the weekend for Lisa and their three children. Even when he was physically present, he was often mentally and emotionally absent.

Lisa, likewise, had replaced her longing for Dusty's attention and affection with a busy social calendar. She had joined the tennis team at the country club. She volunteered at the local elementary school and in the community. It seemed like the only time they spent together as a family was in church on Sunday mornings. Both Dusty and Lisa felt it was a worthwhile commitment, but it had become more obligatory over time. They wanted their children to be exposed to the positive moral messages. Each week, however, they found themselves listening to the sermons, silently hoping that the other would apply the principles taught rather than seeking to grow personally. Even while sitting side by side in the sanctuary, they felt like strangers.

They rarely spoke about anything significant, such as their hopes and dreams or personal needs. The lack of deep emotional connection and intimacy primed the pump for frequent conflict. When they weren't fighting, a constant tension filled the air. Resentment had taken root in their relationship, and daily exchanges were all too often filled with caustic comments and signs of contempt. They demonstrated very little patience toward one another, and worse still, Dusty felt a growing sense of emptiness. Dusty wasn't happy in their relationship, and he knew Lisa wasn't either. They had been sucking the lifeblood out of one another like two leeches locked in a deadly depleting hold. Frankly, he didn't know how much longer they could hold it together—or if he really wanted to anymore.

Pulling into the parking lot, Dusty shifted his thinking to his agenda for the day. He tried to push the cares and concerns about his relationship with Lisa to the back of his mind, but he knew all too well that he couldn't completely separate his personal life from his professional life.

Engaging in these mental gymnastics left him frustrated and negatively impacted his work. He could suppress his pessimistic emotions only so long before they began to spill over into other personal interactions. Nonetheless, he put on his best game face, picked up his pace, and walked into the office with a contrived cheerful demeanor.

After packing a full day into a few hours, he headed to Classic Car Care. He arrived a few minutes early and walked into the waiting area. Fred was seated in one of the leather chairs talking with a customer about vintage trucks. He introduced Dusty to his friend, a car collector who always brought his vehicles to Fred for maintenance. After a brief conversation, the gentleman excused himself and left Dusty and Fred to talk.

"I'm here to get the oil changed in Lisa's car," Dusty said.

"Oh, skip that," Fred retorted. "I checked the records. Unless you've taken several long road trips in the last few weeks, I don't think it's due for a change. Let's walk around the corner and get some coffee!"

"Well, okay." Dusty chuckled under his breath.

He tried to contain his laughter so he wouldn't have to reveal his recent conversation with Lisa. Once at the coffee shop, they both ordered iced coffee and sat at a table on the patio. It was a beautiful spring afternoon. The cool drink offered the perfect balance of refreshment and caffeine to kick-start their conversation. "So to what do I owe the honor of you scheduling an oil change that you really don't need?" Fred asked curiously.

Dusty was busted and a little embarrassed. "Well, I really wanted to continue our conversation about engagement, and I could use a little business advice."

"You want business advice from a mechanic?"

"You've probably forgotten more about running a business than I'll ever know, and I really would like to pick your brain," Dusty said.

"Well, despite what Howard Levine says, I'd like to think I still have a few nuggets of wisdom left to be mined somewhere between my ears. I'd be happy to offer advice where I think it might be helpful, but I won't attempt to bluff you if it's outside my value grade." Dusty had never heard that term before. He knew what a pay grade was, but *value grade*? He asked Fred what he meant by that.

"Life," Fred said, "is all about creating value. The secret to fulfillment is in seeking to bring value to every endeavor. Pay grade speaks to the kind of value you *extract from* the organization. Value grade speaks to the kind of value you *create for* the organization. I'm not talking about posturing or leveraging opportunities for personal gain. That may work for a while, but sooner or later people will figure out that you are all about *you*.

"However, if an employee is always looking to enrich the lives of others or bring added value to the work environment, then their contributions will become evident and their work will be rewarded for what it is—a valuable contribution. When your value grade exceeds your pay grade, you become invaluable—if not indispensable—to the organization. In this case, I promise to do my best to bring value in the area of my strengths, but I won't blow smoke your way if it's beyond my personal knowledge and experience."

> *When your value grade exceeds your pay grade, you become invaluable—if not indispensable—to the organization.*

As Dusty was wrapping his head around that concept, Fred shifted gears. "Now, let's get right to business. Let's talk about your oil change."

"I thought you said the car didn't need an oil change?"

"It doesn't. I'm not talking about Lisa's car. I'm talking about either you or your business, or both. I assume you want to change something or you wouldn't want my advice. Is that correct?"

"Well, yes. But you don't even know what the issues are yet," Dusty said, a bit perplexed.

"I don't have to know the issues to know that you're seeking a change, and in order for change to lead to growth, there must always be an injection of something fresh to keep the parts moving properly without binding," Fred explained. "You want something to shift, and you need fresh 'oil' to make that happen. So let's first talk about change.

"Change is inevitable and always begins with a situation— a clutch situation," Fred said as he took a pen from his freshly pressed shirt pocket and started to write on a napkin.

"Each clutch situation will either lead to personal growth or produce pain. At this pivotal point, we have to make a choice. If we embrace the situation and engage in the change process, then we have the opportunity to grow.

"But if we become defensive and resistant to change, then we forfeit an opportunity for growth and perceive the situation as a hardship. And typically hardships are seen as situations to be endured. How you view the clutch situation depends on your perspective. It's a matter of choice. We have been given the wonderful privilege and opportunity to choose. It is both a personal right and a responsibility. It's what I like to call the either/ or factor. *Either* we choose to resist change and stagnate, *or* we choose to embrace the situation and grow. Choosing to grow leads to transformation, while choosing otherwise leads to degeneration. You see, we all get to make our own choices freely in life, up to a certain point—and then our

We all get to make our own choices freely in life, up to a certain point— and then our choices begin to make us!

44

choices begin to make us! Ultimately, we all become the product of our choices."

"What exactly do you mean?" Dusty asked.

"Take the situation with Lisa's car. Let's say it did need an oil change. You know you need to change the oil, but you never make the choice and take the action necessary to change it. You could, but you justify your lack of action. You may claim that you're too busy. You rationalize that it will be all right to go a little longer. It's inconvenient to slow down from your other obligations to address it. You have multiple opportunities, but you still don't make the right choice to change it. Sooner or later that choice will catch up with you. After a while, you may throw a rod and then the engine will freeze up. Now the choice not to change your oil has begun to shape your future. It has left you with another choice—a more expensive choice. Now you have to choose to replace the engine or buy another vehicle. Sure, the right choice may have cost you a little time and money initially, but it would have kept you on the road.

"I see people all the time in life and in business making choices that limit their futures. Poor choices narrow your options, while good choices open a whole new vista of opportunities. Let me show you how that works."

Fred sketched on the napkin as he continued to talk.

"Let's talk about the upward spiral of growth, or what I like to call 'shifting into growth gear.' When a clutch situation arises and we choose to embrace it, that situation becomes an opportunity to seek and apply new truths. And truth applied leads to transformation.

"The 'oil' that makes shifting into growth gear possible without grinding is humility. Humility allows us to see ourselves honestly, without pretense, and leads to greater self-awareness. Humility is an acknowledgment of our humanity. It is the awareness that we are not perfect and have no need to posture ourselves as being perfect. We all have room to grow. Unfortunately, many people are stunted in their growth because they are self-deluded, believing things about themselves that simply are not true. Rather than embracing change, they resist and try to posture themselves in a flattering light."

Dusty's thoughts immediately shifted to Trey, one of his team leaders. Trey was young and enthusiastic with contagious energy and unquestioned commitment. The problem, however, was that his superiors thought he was uncoachable. Every time someone offered a suggestion that might improve his performance, Trey was dismissive and chose his own solution instead. When challenged, he often became defensive and was prone to deflect responsibility to others when things didn't turn out as planned. Dusty had high hopes for Trey, but he also knew that many of those around him were growing weary of his know-it-all attitude.

Humility allows us to see ourselves honestly, without pretense, and leads to greater self-awareness.

Dusty quickly refocused on the conversation at hand.

"Without honesty and humility, valucentricity is virtually impossible," Fred continued.

Dusty had no idea what Fred meant by valucentricity, but he didn't want to interrupt Fred's train of thought.

"Self-awareness comes through honest introspection and evaluation. A healthy evaluation of a situation causes us to see ourselves as we truly are and to weigh the options and potential outcomes of our actions. It forces us to stop and consider the factors involved. Candid evaluation launches us on a journey to seek truth. But the extent to which we find truth is directly proportionate to our openness and willingness to receive it. There is a proverbial saying that goes like this: 'When the student is ready, the teacher will appear.' Dusty, the answers to your questions are within your reach. They always have been. But you have to ask the questions before you can receive the answers. You are finally beginning to ask."

Dusty thought Fred was beginning to sound more like a Buddhist monk than a business advisor. But he suspended his judgment and let Fred go on.

"Once you ask, you open yourself up to receiving answers. The funny thing is that so many people never ask profound questions. Maybe they feel that asking is a sign of weakness. They pretend to have all the answers themselves. It could be that by not asking, they feel more self-sufficient. Whatever the reason, it is almost always driven by pride. And pride always appears before a fall."

"So, ask and you shall receive," Dusty quipped, with an edge of sarcasm in his tone.

"In a way, yes!" Fred responded. "You see, Dusty, you are always going to receive something from somebody. The question becomes, 'Receive what from whom?' There will always be an abundance of people eager to offer their opinions. You have to determine to whom you will listen and what you will receive. A good student learns best by asking the right questions and then selecting wisely whom he will allow to provide him with the answers. It's really pretty simple. You must choose carefully. Good counsel perpetuates good choices.

Bad counsel perpetuates bad choices. Good counsel amplifies valucentricity. Bad counsel short-circuits valucentricity."

There was that term again.

Fred continued. "One of the keys to growth is asking great questions. If you ask poor questions, you're likely to get poor answers. If you ask good questions, you're likely to get good answers. But if you ask profound questions and are willing to listen with humility, then often you'll get profound answers.

You are always going to receive something from somebody. The question becomes, "Receive what from whom?"

"Let's say that something has gone wrong with a project at work. As you convene the team and bring the situation to the table, a poor question might be, 'Who is to blame for getting us into this mess?' or 'Why did it happen?' Poor questions usually revolve around problems and personalities. Frequently, they're attempts to shift blame or get people to see things from our perspective and side with us. They involve posturing. By asking poor questions, you're really seeking to deflect responsibility or affirm your position. The answers may make for lively conversation, but they are never helpful. Even if you successfully assign blame, you're no closer to resolving the problem.

"By asking good questions, however, you can understand exactly what took place. A good question might be something like, 'What went wrong, and how can we prevent it from happening again?' Good questions guide you toward a better understanding of the situation but stop short of getting you to any reasonable resolutions. However, asking profound questions gets you to the heart of the matter. This opens the door for new possibilities because you are able to dissect the dysfunction that led to the problem and then set up a solution. A profound question would be, 'What can we learn from this, and how can we leverage that knowledge to solve the problem?' When you move beyond personalities and problems and shift your thinking to a solution-oriented perspective, you become inspired. Once you get to the solution side, people are much more likely to roll up their sleeves and get to work.

"Growth is inspirational. When people are authentic and open to change, others feel drawn in and inspired to be open and honest as well. Where there is defensiveness and resistance, people pull away from one another and erect emotional barriers. When authenticity and humility are present, unity is often the result. And unity is the most powerful force in the universe for the creation of good. Unity enhances value creation. And it all begins by being honest with yourself about who you are. Humility is the 'oil' that allows you to shift smoothly into growth gear."

As he had been talking, Fred had written three key thoughts, which spiraled up from the clutch situation. Dusty paused to look at each of them and pondered their significance in light of their conversation.

Humility is the "oil" that allows you to shift smoothly into growth gear.

"So," Dusty interjected, "in each clutch situation we have a choice to make. We can adopt an attitude of humility and embrace change, or we can become defensive and resist change. Humility allows us to evaluate the situation and ourselves honestly and shifts us into growth gear. Growth always involves a solution-oriented perspective. And growth creates unity

SHIFTING INTO GROWTH GEAR

UNITY/INSPIRATION

SOLUTION ORIENTATION

HONEST EVALUATION

CLUTCH SITUATION

and inspiration. I get all of that. But what do you mean by *valucentricity?*"

"I was wondering how long it was going to take you to ask me about that. Let me make a quick run to the restroom, and when I get back we can talk about valucentricity," Fred responded.

Fred excused himself and left Dusty to wrestle with his thoughts for a few minutes. The hook was certainly set. Dusty was obviously on the line. He examined the drawing on the napkin until Fred returned.

PART 2

ALIGNMENT

*Far and away the best prize that life has to offer is
the chance to work hard at work worth doing.*
THEODORE ROOSEVELT

5

Valucentricity

Fred returned to the table, ready to reel Dusty into a whole
new way of seeing his situation.

"Value-centric," Fred re-engaged, "simply means that
values are at the very core of who you are and what you do.
Your values determine how you see the world and respond
to it. You could say that values shape a person's worldview.
Valucentricity, then, is the energy and momentum that can be
produced when values are properly aligned. It's like the spark
that ignites the gas to create internal combustion. Think
electricity. Electricity is a type of energy found in nature,
but it can be man-made as well. Likewise, there is a natural
structure of value in the universe. When we intentionally
choose to align values, those values create a circuit through
which power can flow. When we understand value alignment
and value creation, we can craft movements of good through
which positive energy can flow to light up the world."

"I think I'm following you. Please go on," Dusty prompted.

"Well, each person sees the world through a unique lens, which is crafted by the prioritization of certain values. Have you ever wondered how two people can experience the same situation and come away from it with two totally different interpretations of the event? You see, we can choose to 'spin' reality any way we want, depending on what we choose to emphasize. That's what I call subjective reality. Think of the politician whose positions constantly morph to match the changing winds of the polls. They are choosing to create their own reality. Or, more accurately stated, they're letting the opinions of others shape their reality. That subjective reality cannot last for long. Sooner or later objective reality—which is inescapable and cannot be spun—will emerge. And when it does, a person's character is revealed through their values. Such a person might value power or popularity more highly than integrity. Whatever the case, their values are distorted and will eventually expose their judgment. Or as some in the South are fond of saying, 'Whatever is down in your well will eventually come up in your bucket!'

Valucentricity, then, is the energy and momentum that can be produced when values are properly aligned.

"The more closely your subjective reality aligns with objective reality, the healthier, happier, and more resilient you will be. In organizational life, if your values align with those of others, then greater synergy and positive energy will result. There is great power in identifying, clarifying, and aligning values. That power is valucentricity.

"You see, a person's values are the most accurate predictor of what will come up in their bucket. There's actually a science called *axiology* that is dedicated to understanding how values shape a person's perspective on life and work. It is the study of values and value formation and how they impact our thought processes, decision-making skills, and performance. The father of modern axiology, Dr. Robert S. Hartman, postulated that all of our choices are value-driven. According to him, values form the foundation for all human behavior. Hartman dedicated his life to defining and studying the concept of *good*. For him, something was good if it possessed all the properties necessary to fulfill its purpose. Good, according to Hartman, is about fulfilling one's personal po-

Good, then, is defined as functioning fully and effectively to maximize your strengths, passions, and capabilities. As such, the creation of good could be considered humanity's most lofty pursuit.

tential. It has more to do with pursuing excellence than it does with success. Success is often measured in comparison to what others have done, which is always a self-defeating proposition.

"Good, however, is about the pursuit of excellence—comparing yourself to your capabilities and seeking to become all you were meant to be. Good, then, is defined as functioning fully and effectively to maximize your strengths, passions, and capabilities. As such, the creation of good could be considered humanity's most lofty pursuit. Hartman was consumed with the idea that good could actually be measured and that movements of good could be created by applying certain principles."

Dusty had never heard of axiology. But what Fred was saying about values driving behavior certainly made sense. Dusty wondered how he could have completed his postgraduate studies and never have heard of such a science. He took out his phone and made a note to do some research on axiology and Robert Hartman.

Then he asked Fred, "So how did you become familiar with axiology?"

"Ah . . . for that, I forever will be indebted to my good friend and former roommate, Howie. At his insistence, we rented an apartment in New Haven, Connecticut, and enrolled in a summer course under Dr. Hartman when he was a visiting professor at Yale. We both became enamored with his teachings and the principles of axiology that could be applied to craft a more compelling corporate culture."

That was all Dusty needed to hear. Fred's testimonial was convincing, but the fact that Howard Levine had used the same principles solidified Dusty's resolve to learn as much as he could about axiology.

"So valucentricity is power produced through alignment of strong morals?" asked Dusty.

"A person's morals are definitely part of the equation," Fred responded, "but there's more to it than that. Your moral values will certainly find expression in your daily decisions. Let me see if I can explain it more clearly. It may make more sense to say that valucentricity refers to the energy that can be created when you place the proper emphasis on certain aspects of life. It's about alignment of one's perspective and priorities. When we speak of values, we often think of ethical values—those deeply held personal convictions that typically have a spiritual foundation. We may think of ethical values in terms of what is right, moral, and just. But there are also values that are more functional in nature.

"These values represent trade-offs people make based on what's deemed most important or what holds the highest value for that individual. These values impact how people view themselves and the world, as well as how they relate to others. It can be said that 'how we *view* things will drive how we *do* things.'

"Another way of expressing it is to say that a person's values are the result of how they prioritize certain aspects of life and work. By assessing the value someone places on different elements, we gain insight and understanding as to how that individual likely functions. Understanding one's values provides a framework for effective human interaction. It also forms the foundation of an individual's judgment capacity. So, as I said earlier, the more our personal values align with the natural structure of value in the universe, the healthier and more productive we will be as human beings. Thus, alignment generates valucentricity."

> *How we* view *things will drive how we* do *things.*

"Now you're really starting to sound like a spiritual advisor," Dusty interjected.

"Ah, maybe so, Grasshopper!" Fred whispered with a smile. "There certainly is a spiritual component to valucentricity. Most religions are grounded in the ideals of treating others with honor, dignity, and respect while doing everything within one's power to fulfill their God-given potential. At the same time, clarity and proper alignment of values provide the foundation for someone to live on purpose."

"Live on purpose?" Dusty asked.

"Yes," Fred responded. "Live on purpose. Living on purpose means you live purposefully, with a purpose, and for a purpose. *For a purpose* defines the *what*. It answers the question, 'To what end?' To be remarkable, this *what* must be larger than self, providing a focus that is outward in nature and creates value for others. *With purpose* is about the *how*. It speaks to the passion, enthusiasm, and creativity that one brings to the effort. It is the intensity *with* which a person pursues the *what*.

> *Living on purpose means you live purposefully, with a purpose, and for a purpose.*

And purposefully implies both inspiration and intentionality. It is the *why*. It provides the motivation, because the *why* brings meaning and significance to any endeavor. At its core, purpose defines the *what*, the *how*, and the *why* of any noteworthy activity. And, I might add, purpose is always value-based, because it is the deepest expression of that which one holds most dear. So living on purpose means that one is purposeful in the approach, passionate and undeterred about a purpose, and focused on a purpose beyond self.

"Living on purpose involves assuming personal responsibility for your own thoughts, feelings, and actions. So many people simply drift through life being swept away by circumstances. Living on purpose is living with intentionality. It's life by design, not by default. It's about thinking for yourself and learning how to live above your circumstances. Rather than being negatively influenced by your environment, you are determined to influence your environment in positive ways. This sense of ownership adds clarity and quality to your decision-making processes. When you live on purpose, you fully own your choices and take responsibility for your actions. Simply stated, you no longer fall prey to 'The Other

Guy Syndrome'—that tendency to blame others for your circumstances," Fred said.

"I know exactly what you mean about 'The Other Guy Syndrome,'" Dusty chimed in. "I have a friend who is a defense attorney. He says that most of the people in prison are innocent according to their own testimony. He laughs when he says that the overwhelming majority of those currently incarcerated would be released if only we could catch 'The Other Guy!'"

"Exactly." Fred chuckled as he continued. "But when you live on purpose, you don't blame other people for your actions or excuse them because of the circumstances. You exert the power and the will to live out your values consistently. And when your values are clearly defined and aligned, your convictions rather than your circumstances define your behavior. You are no longer dependent on the actions of others to guide you and make you happy. Nor is your emotional well-being dependent on environmental conditions. Confidence and peace begin to mark your life as you take control of your inner world.

"Living on purpose is living by design, not by default.

"Stress, however, is created when you do not live out your values consistently," Fred continued. "Stress is ever-present, but it's worsened when your actions do not align with your beliefs. This creates what psychologists call cognitive dissonance, which occurs when someone tries to reconcile two elements that are incompatible. This creates turmoil in the mind and heart and robs a person of a sense of peace and harmony. But that's enough for now. We've been treading in deep water long enough for our first swimming lesson.

"My, how time flies when you're on a soapbox," Fred quipped. "Let's pick up the conversation here next time.

That is, if you are interested in exploring the topic a little further."

"You'd be willing to meet again?"

"Sure, as long as you don't try to schedule another unnecessary oil change," Fred chided.

"Could you carve out an hour next Thursday?" Dusty asked, immediately trying to seize Fred's offer.

"Same time next week—you got it," Fred said, sporting his irrepressible grin.

6

On Purpose

When the Employee Engagement Task Force convened again on Tuesday morning, Dusty was ready. He'd done his homework. His head was racing with thoughts and ideas. He felt as if he'd been drinking water from a fire hose the past few days while doing his research, and he knew his colleagues wouldn't respond well if he acted like he'd found a magic potion. He was fully aware that he'd have to introduce some of his ideas slowly to avoid ruffling the feathers of those who were emotionally attached to the status quo.

Jim opened the meeting with a few words of introduction to tee up the discussion. "When we last met, I asked you to apply your best thinking to this issue of engagement. As I said, we need to figure out who and what we want to become and then take the necessary measures to inspire the best in our people! We are going to have to shift our thinking if we are to fulfill our potential. How are we going to do that?" he asked. "The floor is open for your observations and suggestions. I'm counting on this conversation to spark our imaginations. Let's do some creative brainstorming and good work today."

Jim's words reverberated in Dusty's head. His mind began to make word associations. When Jim said "shift," Dusty immediately thought *getting into growth gear*. When Jim said "good," Dusty thought *fulfilling one's personal potential— pursuing excellence*. He was beginning to scare himself with how quickly thoughts were coming to his mind, so he decided to scribble a few notes while others spoke first.

The ensuing conversation followed the familiar course. There was talk about those areas that received low scores in the survey. Then there was the usual banter about which issues, if addressed effectively, could provide the greatest lift. This was followed by an emotional conversation about what had and had not worked in the past. Lines were being drawn and defenses were being erected.

Ann Marie, one of Dusty's counterparts, was particularly troubled. Like others, she had grown frustrated with her inability to find meaningful solutions. She questioned whether or not engagement could be measured effectively and if any corporate interventions could produce significant results. While she was not alone in her thinking, her negativity was palpable and evident in many of her interactions with others throughout the organization. She was prone to see life and work through darkly tinted glasses and seldom offered hopeful feedback. Her pointed comments were creating a quagmire. The whole conversation was being bogged down.

Dusty felt like he was on a merry-go-round that, at first, was spinning too fast but now was grinding to a halt. His body language must have given him away because Jim brought him directly into the middle of the fray with a question.

"Dusty, you've been uncharacteristically quiet. What thoughts do you have to offer about all of this?"

Dusty took a deep breath and swallowed. He wasn't uncomfortable speaking his mind, but he wanted to temper his words so that they would have the most impact.

"My thoughts run along two lines. First, when it comes to engagement, I wonder if we are measuring the right things. Many of the survey questions are designed to determine how satisfied folks are with certain environmental factors. I, for one, am not sure that is an accurate reflection of engagement. A stronger indicator of engagement may be a healthy assessment of our culture. Culture is the collective expression of the values, beliefs, and behaviors that individuals bring to the organization. Culture is *who you are* as a company—not *what you have* or even *what you do*. If the culture is healthy, then high engagement is almost certain. Engagement is simply a symptom of an organization's cultural condition.

"Engagement is often defined as the emotional attachment people feel toward an organization or endeavor. I've come to believe that a person's emotional attachment to their work will be determined by whether or not their personal values align with organizational values. There is great power in the alignment of values, or what one might call valucentricity. Valucentricity creates synergy, by which movements of good can be created.

"Also, if we're really trying to 'engage, empower, and enrich' our associates' lives, then perhaps we should do less for them and equip them to do more for themselves. What if, instead of tolerating less-than-stellar environmental conditions, our people began to assume responsibility for positively impacting their environments? Rather than passively conforming to the surroundings, they would become agents of change. How might encouraging them to take more initiative in creating value impact the work environment? Empowering our people by teaching them to live on purpose—which is simply living intentionally and assuming personal responsibility for their own thoughts, feelings, and actions—could be revolutionary."

"All right, you have our attention," Jim said, "but can you unpack those ideas a little more and help us wrap our minds around them?"

"Well, think of your favorite philanthropic organization. It probably has a significant number of volunteers who freely give their time, energy, and resources to help the organization. Many of those people make significant sacrifices simply for the sake of the cause. In corporate ranks, we use money as a primary motivator. But in a volunteer organization, compensation is not even a factor. That kind of passionate commitment and discretionary effort is the result of an alignment of values. They believe deeply in a mission and feel called to align with a cause. I think there is much we could learn from studying volunteer organizations. Understanding how values influence human behavior and the power that can be harnessed by identifying and properly aligning values could be truly transformational.

"I wonder how many suboptimal environmental conditions might be changed for the better or rendered nonfactors if we truly tapped into the passion of our people. Rather than developing costly corporate initiatives, what if we helped team members more clearly define and live out their values?

What if we empowered them to think about life and work differently? What if we taught our associates how to make decisions based on conviction rather than on convenience? And what if we tapped into their strengths and passions to energize their work every day? I wonder what might happen if team members saw themselves as change agents for good?"

Dusty was on a roll. He was beginning to feel like an impassioned preacher. The only problem was that he had exhausted the content of his sermon. There was a pause. Then Anne Marie asked the inevitable question: "How do you suggest we do that?"

The question was followed by a lengthy, awkward silence. While he flipped through his notes, Dusty frantically scoured his brain for information he had gleaned from Fred and his research. No answers came to mind. Finally, Jim came to his rescue.

"I think we may be onto something here. I'm anxious to hear how you might suggest we put legs to some of these concepts. I have to tell you that I'm intrigued with the ideas of valucentricity and living on purpose. If I understand correctly, purposeful living could be described as living out your values in a mature and meaningful way. I like that.

"I'm bothered by the immaturity I see in some of our associates that I would describe as an attitude of entitlement. There seems to be a general expectation of getting more in exchange for doing less. If we are going to survive, then this has to change. Dusty, I want to hear your thoughts about how all of this might play out in our corporate context. Can you come back to next Tuesday's meeting with a formal presentation?"

Now I've done it, Dusty thought. He had opened Pandora's box. However, he was not one to challenge the status

67

quo without offering suggestions for improvement. *Besides,* he thought, *although Pandora released all manner of evil into the world, at least she retained the angel of Hope.* Dusty was hopeful that maybe this time around they could move the compass needle northward, so he agreed to bring his thoughts to the table. Then, as quickly as he voiced his commitment, he began to panic. Thankfully, knowing he would see Fred again in two days helped keep his feelings in control. By the time Thursday afternoon rolled around, Dusty was armed and ready to bombard Fred with questions.

7

Creativity

Fred came moseying into the coffee shop at four o'clock in his usual khakis and pressed shirt with the Classic Car Care logo emblazoned on the pocket. Dusty had arrived early. He had one hour of Fred's time and was determined to make the most of it. He had ordered them both drinks and was waiting at a table with his notebook open and his pen poised. Before Fred could sit down, Dusty fired his first question: "So how do you teach someone to live on purpose?"

"Good afternoon to you too, Dusty." Fred chuckled. "I see that you're ready to receive some answers."

"I'm sorry," Dusty responded. "It's just that I'm eager to understand how everything you've shared might apply to my situation at work. I've done some homework and have come to believe that some of the principles found in axiology might just be the ticket to help us significantly improve our corporate culture. As I understand it, a person's values explain how they view and respond to the world."

"Sounds like you *have* done your homework!" Fred replied. "Let's get to your question. As I said last time, living on purpose is about choosing to live above your circumstances. To do that, you have to understand the maxims that guide value creation.

"First," said Fred, "we have to talk about the Maxim of Creativity. *Maxim* isn't a commonly used word, but it has wonderful implications. A maxim is a general truth, a principle, or a rule of conduct. Think of a maxim as the best means to *maxim*ize your performance. And this first maxim is foundational. The Maxim of Creativity is about value creation. As human beings, we are designed to create value in life. There are essentially two approaches to life: one seeks to *extract value from* every endeavor, and the other seeks to *create and bring value to* every endeavor. Some might say you have 'givers' and 'takers,' but it's not quite that simple.

"You see, healthy people want to grow. By nature, they want to improve and establish a sense of self-mastery. They accept responsibility for themselves and their futures. This emphasis on personal responsibility is the antithesis of en-titlement. As people and organizations mature, so does a desire to make a positive contribution to the world and those immediately around us. We want our presence to make a positive difference. We want to be appreciated and affirmed for our work. We want to leave a lasting legacy. But this de-sire to bring value can often become twisted into a drive to achieve. Some people think life is defined and measured by pay scale and material possessions. It's the same mentality that says, 'He who dies with the most toys wins.' For some people, success is all about titles and trinkets. But that's a perversion of a natural longing for significance that comes through creating value.

"A sense of satisfaction and significance comes from understanding who you are and how you can best bring value to every relationship and every endeavor in life. This is where people in the 'self-esteem movement' have jumped the tracks and seriously derailed many young lives, while mistakenly trying to protect the tender egos of our young people. In an attempt to prevent kids from feeling inadequate due to comparisons, competition has been effectively removed from many youth sports programs. After all, to have a winner necessitates that you have a loser, and nobody should be referred to as the loser—at least according to this line of thinking. Therefore, no scores are kept in these athletic leagues. But don't be fooled. The kids always know who wins the game! Likewise, everyone receives the same trophy or ribbon, no matter how well or how poorly they play. In other words, everyone is rewarded for nothing more than showing up. As a result, we now have far too many young people emerging in the marketplace who want to be rewarded for simply showing up! We call this attitude *entitlement*. But it's not altogether their fault. We set them up for it."

> **The Maxim of Creativity**
>
> *We are designed to create value in life. There are essentially two approaches to life: one seeks to* extract value from *every endeavor, and the other seeks to* create and bring value to *every endeavor.*

"I see where you're going with this," Dusty said. "It's not that we should teach our kids to win at any cost, but in real life we are rewarded according to our performance and contribution. It's important to teach our kids to win with grace and lose with dignity. And a sense of responsibility encourages them to take the steps necessary to improve rather than motivating them to expect others to run to their rescue or reward them for poor performance."

"Precisely!" Fred affirmed. "Losing is part of life. Sooner or later, everyone is going to experience a loss. It's how you deal with it that really counts. Your losses don't have to define you. The people I know who possess the greatest character have overcome their losses and challenges to rise victoriously on the other side. What we really need to teach our kids is that a healthy self-esteem comes from a healthy sense of self-worth. And self-worth comes from the conviction that you are a person of great value and the confidence of knowing you've made a significant contribution to a good cause. In other words, self-worth comes from knowing you have created value."

> *Self-worth comes from the conviction that you are a person of great value and the confidence of knowing you've made a significant contribution to a good cause. In other words, self-worth comes from knowing you have created value.*

"I would assume that ideally those who bring the greatest value to an organization should be compensated and rewarded for their contributions in order to share in the value they have created," Dusty ventured. "That value creation could come in the form of revenue generation, stellar service, or the sharing of best practices. It might even be the value brought by those who have contributed the most in terms of collaboration or innovation."

"Yes," responded Fred, "but let me take it a step further. What we are looking for is valucentricity. Let's say that your top sales producer is also a real prima donna. He may generate revenue, but his attitude is cancerous. His presence may be *extracting as much value from* the team as he is *creating and bringing value to* the team through his sales efforts. The money he makes can never take priority over the way he treats people. Strong organizations always put people ahead of profits because they know that if you do right by your people—internally and externally—then the profits will follow. Therefore, the person who provides the greatest valucentricity is the person who brings both productivity and positive energy to the environment. In every situation, we have a choice to make—we can either seek to create value or seek to extract value. Fulfillment comes through creating as much value as possible. Does that make sense?"

"Absolutely, and it gives me a whole new way of evaluating each situation. It makes me think of all the metrics we use in the call center. Trust me when I say we know how to *do* metrics! We are a production-oriented, metrics-driven, spreadsheet-proliferating organization. When it comes to metrics, you could say we are militant. But the one thing we have not been able to accurately assess is the passion of our people. And we certainly haven't done anything to help our associates take full responsibility for their attitudes and contributions. Instead, we keep beating our heads against the wall trying to figure out what we can give them that will make them happier. Now I realize that the best thing we can give them is an opportunity to utilize our mission and vision to create value through a worthy endeavor. If I understand you correctly, energy levels will increase as people see that they are creating value for others and working toward a worthy cause."

"It sounds like you're getting it," Fred said. "Now let me ask you a question."

"Fire away."

"How do most organizations approach value engineering?" asked Fred.

Dusty thought for a moment and then offered the perfect textbook answer. "Value engineering is based on function and cost analysis. It's an attempt to get a better product to market faster and cheaper than competitors."

"All right, that's a spot-on definition," Fred acknowledged. "Given those three adjectives—better, faster, and cheaper—which one is emphasized most often?"

"In my experience, the focus is almost always on cheaper. Cutting costs is typically seen as the clearest path to increasing margin for the producer or service provider and value for the customer."

"That's what I've witnessed most often as well," Fred said. "However, that approach stifles valucentricity. It takes no genius to cut costs. In the absence of creative energy, the default position is always to eliminate expenses. However, valucentricity is generated by focusing on creating such a remarkable product or service for the customer that you deliver an experience worth repeating. And remarkable experiences have more to do with personal attention than price point.

"If your focus is purely on numbers, then the question becomes, 'How low can we drive our costs before our customers will no longer tolerate the quality of our product or the level of service we provide?' But if your focus is on crafting a memorable experience, then the question becomes,

'How can we create so much value that our products and services become remarkable?' Remarkable means we interact with others in such a way that we leave them with an irrepressible desire to talk about their encounter with us. You see, valucentricity emphasizes making a difference over making a dollar. That difference is found in making meaningful emotional connections with people. If you successfully make those connections, then

Valucentricity emphasizes making a difference over making a dollar.

your customers will happily pay full price for your services because they perceive you as offering more value. Every organization creates transactions. But great organizations create powerful relationships through the superior value they bring to the table.

"You see, relationships trump transactions every time. And when the value you provide exceeds all expectations, people will talk about it. You become remarkable. Robert Stephens, founder of Geek Squad, was fond of saying, 'Advertising is the tax you pay for being unremarkable.'"

"Wow, that's really good," Dusty said. "Word of mouth is always the most powerful way for your message to be spread. And I see now that the relationship makes the referral powerful. At the same time, value engineering should be more value conscious than cost conscious. Because the moment you concentrate on price, you've lost your creative edge. Focusing on numbers unplugs you from the power of valucentricity. Numbers will not produce value. Value produces numbers."

"I couldn't have said it better myself."

Dusty's thoughts wandered once again to Query. For years, the company had tried to drive productivity by increasing the number of calls each specialist fielded. Scripts had been carefully crafted to eliminate small talk, and call times were monitored to the second. Everyone was incentivized to *close* as many calls as possible within each time block. As a result, the number of calls handled increased steadily, but customer satisfaction trended in the opposite direction. Now Dusty began to wonder what might happen if they threw away the scripts and encouraged their specialists to make a genuine relational connection with each customer, listening carefully to their needs instead of trying to steer them toward a quick but unsatisfactory solution.

He immediately realized that they would have to increase the number of specialists in order for each caller to receive such undivided attention. The costs could be enormous. At the same time, Dusty knew it wasn't uncommon for a customer to call two or three times or to be transferred multiple times in an attempt to resolve a single issue. Taking more time with each customer might actually reduce the number of calls they would have to field. It almost certainly would improve customer satisfaction. And he couldn't help but think about how much more rewarding it would be for team members if they felt connected to each customer.

8

Positivity

"Like you just said, a person's energy level increases as the individual creates value." Fred's words brought Dusty back from his meandering thoughts.

"The Maxim of Positivity explains just how that happens. It states that authentic positivity is the by-product of creating true value. By positivity I'm not referring to a Pollyanna attitude toward life or fluff or what some might describe as self-help hype. On the contrary, as we create true value for others, positive energy and emotion are natural by-products of our actions. Positivity and valucentricity are synonymous. And value creation answers the question, 'How does someone experience the good in life?'"

Fred leaned in and asked, "Have you ever noticed how happiness is so elusive? Literally, the harder you pursue it, the more frustrated you become. Sir John Templeton said, 'Happiness pursued, eludes; happiness given, returns.' The same could be said for success. Some of the most success-ful people often don't think they are successful. That's why they often chase their own tails to exhaustion. It's really very sad. The more you seek to be fulfilled, the less you actually experience fulfillment. That's because these 'good' aspects are not ends in themselves or goals to be attained but rather by-products of creating value.

"From a corporate perspective, think about innovation. Innovation and the ability to adapt to a changing market-place are essential to any organization's survival. However, the more a company attempts to systematize efficiency in the pursuit of innovation, the less likely that organization will experience great measures of it. The more structure, policies, and procedures an organization puts in place to pursue innovation and the more pressure that's applied to produce it, the less likely it will occur. This is because pressure drains emotional energy that could and should be applied to nurture creativity. When that energy is siphoned off by rigid dictates and demands, the gravitational forces of efficiency keep the imagination earthbound.

The Maxim of Positivity

Authentic positivity is the by-product of creating true value.

"The applied principles of Scientific Management, as set forth by Frederick Taylor, can actually quell innovation if one is not careful. Efficiency pressed to the extreme can minimize the human element. That's not to say there aren't disciplines that must be utilized in the creative processes. On the contrary, innovation requires the disciplines of slowing, observing, and questioning. Each of these takes time. Time that is necessary for reflection and meditation on the 'what ifs' and 'why nots.'

The idea of taking time for reflection is counterintuitive and flies in the face of process efficiency. But the reality is that if you want to create an environment of innovation, then you need to give people time to think and dream—while on the clock. Give them the opportunity and resources to work on a solution to a problem or to come up with a service that's of interest to them—something they really want to work on in an area where they can create the greatest value. The stated objective of this discretionary time should always be to employ their passion and their strengths to bring as much value to the organization as they possibly can. Then step back and watch innovation take place."

While Fred was talking, Dusty's mind took a tour of all the failed corporate initiatives floated down from on high at Query. Then he thought about a community service project that a few people in one of the call centers had initiated and championed. They had successfully rallied both the people and the resources to begin the project. In just two years, it had grown into an annual two-day event in which people from across the organization volunteered time in the community to work with local shelters and food banks. It had gained so much momentum that corporate had embraced it. Everyone in the Atlanta offices had become involved.

"Success," Fred continued, "comes in much the same way. When I was in college, I thought the route to success was to get the highest GPA and build the best resume in the hopes of getting the highest-paying job. I planned to extract as much value as I could from the firm that hired me. And it worked—for a season. I was hired by a midsize technology firm and began to move up the corporate ranks. I was making good money, but I wasn't enjoying myself. So I did what so many others do—I sold out to the next highest bidder. Someone was willing to pay me more money, so I switched teams. I became a mercenary in the marketplace. I wasn't any happier in the next role. But I justified the move by convincing myself that if I was going to be miserable doing what I was doing, at least I was going to make more money doing it. Of course, making more money didn't do anything to brighten my spirits or bring more enjoyment to my work. My entire focus was on extracting value rather than creating value.

"So many people enter the marketplace today with the same mentality. Success for them is all about getting a high-paying job. It has little to do with enjoying the work or whether or not their values align with the organization. It has less to do with passion and purpose than it does with the paycheck. As a result, they see themselves as free agents rather than long-term team members or employees. They sign on for a single season and then evaluate their position based on a variety of conditions that are all framed by value extraction. You could call it a spirit of entitlement. Whatever you choose to call it, the decision has little to do with creating value and everything to do with 'what's in it for me?'"

Dusty began to squirm in his chair, growing increasingly uncomfortable with the course of the conversation. Fred's recollection of his career sounded very similar to Dusty's corporate journey. There had been many times in the past few years that Dusty had actually asked himself why he was doing what he was doing. He didn't interrupt Fred, but he hoped the rest of the story would be a bit brighter.

"Then Howie came along, and everything changed for me. He offered me a partnership in a start-up company. I jumped at the opportunity to work with him. By that time,

Howie was committed to applying the principles of value creation in day-to-day business. We began to craft our talent development initiatives and best practices around these very principles. We had a blast growing the company and its culture. And I dare say we created an environment where people enjoyed working because they saw the value they brought to the lives of our clients and, consequently, to the organization.

"Within twelve years we had garnered significant market share and the attention of our peers in the industry. When we were offered the opportunity to sell, we struggled with letting others come in and potentially change our model. As part of the negotiations, we were both asked to stay on for a two-year transitional period to ensure that the culture would be perpetuated. We agreed. We continued to grow the company for those two years and then made our exit. Howie went on to his next gig, and I made enough money to retire. It was exactly what I had wanted to do since I had planned my career path back in college. I was forty-one and retired! Being young and retired was incredible—for about six months.

"That's when I really experienced the full impact of value creation. As the Maxim of Creativity states, we were designed to create value. I bored quickly of playing golf three times a week and going on solo fishing trips. It wasn't long before Anne started kicking me out of the house because I was getting on her nerves. Then it dawned on me. I was miserable because I wasn't creating the kind of value that I knew I was capable of creating. So I hoisted the flag and flew my colors again. Before I knew it, Performax, the company that had purchased us less than three years earlier, asked me to take over at the helm. It was a great run, and I had the time of my life. When I finally stepped down eight years ago, I opened up Classic Car Care. The fact is that I will never retire. S. Truett Cathy, the founder of Chick-fil-A, once said, 'Learn to love your work and you'll never have to "work" again.' I sincerely believe that. Now I play with cars three days a week and get paid for it. The rest of my time is spent with Anne and the grandkids and serving on the boards of three philanthropic organizations. And in each of these arenas, I seek to bring as much value to the table as I can.

....

"Learn to love your work and you'll never have to 'work' again."

S. Truett Cathy, founder of Chick-fil-A

....

"Like I said, I have discovered that success is a by-product of creating value. Happiness is a by-product of creating value. Significance is a by-product of creating value. Fulfillment is a by-product of creating value. I would even say that courage and optimism are by-products of creating value. We were designed to create value. You can create value organizationally, and you can create value interpersonally. Creating value in relationships engenders trust and openness. It breeds camaraderie among colleagues. It fosters goodwill. It heals hurts. It offers forgiveness and second chances. At the same time, it holds people accountable for bringing their very best to the table in every endeavor."

Dusty wondered how this all might apply to his relationship with his seventeen-year-old son, Mike. Because Mike was the eldest of Dusty and Lisa's three children, they had especially high expectations of him. In moments of honest reflection, Dusty acknowledged that he had pushed Mike pretty hard to excel in just about everything from academics to sports and summer internships. Mike was a junior in high school and had always done well, but he was beginning to show signs of rebellion. Although Dusty saw him as being gifted, he often thought Mike was lazy and would voice his disappointment in heavily critical ways. Lately it had become clear that Mike was carrying resentment toward him. He frequently spoke disrespectfully to him and to Lisa. And when Dusty reacted with heavy-handed disciplinary measures, it only made matters worse. Mike would either lash out in return or withdraw from the family and shut out Dusty entirely. He wondered what it might look like to create value in his relationship with his son. If there was one thing their relationship obviously needed, it was positivity. Maybe these principles were as important in life as in work.

PART 3

ADJUSTMENT

Our greatest fear should not be of failure but of succeeding at things in life that don't really matter.

FRANCIS CHAN

9

Sustainability

"So is that enough for today, or do you want to continue?" Fred asked. "It's almost five o'clock, and I want to be sensitive to your time."

"You certainly have my attention. I'd like to continue if you don't mind. How many more maxims are there?"

"Two more! Let's discuss them, and then we can call it a day."

"That sounds great to me," Dusty replied.

"The third is the Maxim of Sustainability. It states that to continuously create value, you must leverage your passion and strengths to solve problems. This principle is vital but often misunderstood, so let me break it down. There is a lot of white noise today about pursuing your passion. Motivational speakers are forever encouraging people to 'do what you love to do and the money will follow.' This is a misguided notion. I love to hit the little white ball, but I could never play golf for a living. Nobody would be foolish enough to pay me to play. I simply don't have the game. The reality is that if you do what you love and someone pays you to do it, then great, you call that a job. However, if you do what you love and nobody pays you to do it, then it's nothing more than a hobby.

"Most people don't have the luxury of simply pursuing a passion. It's erroneous and dangerous to encourage people to limit their activity to 'doing what they love to do.' Few people can make a living that way. However, it's vital that people *learn* to 'love what they do.' For some, that may sound like splitting hairs, but it's far more than semantics. People must connect emotionally with their work for it to be meaningful. And making that connection falls largely on the shoulders of leadership. Good leaders inspire those around them to see the value in what they do. They work hard to ensure that personal values are aligned with corporate values. When they are aligned, people develop an emotional attachment to their work. Inspirational leaders also connect the organizational objectives to personal passion. When people are emotionally engaged in their work, they're much more likely to offer discretionary effort. Loyalty, morale, and performance all increase when team members are highly engaged. People need to see that they're making a difference in the lives of others and contributing positively to the world. Sometimes that process begins by reframing someone's perspective of work."

....

The Maxim of Sustainability

To continuously create value, you must leverage your passion and strengths to solve problems.

....

"How do you get employees to reframe their perspective?" Dusty asked.

"By changing the way someone looks at the work experience. Howard Schultz, the CEO of Starbucks, said, 'We're in the people business serving coffee, not the coffee business serving people.' This shift in emphasis changes the paradigm. It's not merely inspirational; it's revolutionary.

> *"We're in the people business serving coffee, not the coffee business serving people."*
>
> Howard Schultz,
> CEO of Starbucks

"Obviously, work should provide a product, service, or solution. But, ultimately, it's about people and somehow making their lives better. When we see our lives as instrumental in creating value for others, the work itself becomes much more meaningful."

"But isn't that just a head game? I mean, after all, that's really nothing more than mental smoke and mirrors," Dusty said cynically.

"I'm not talking about denying or distorting reality. I'm talking about redefining work so that the individual is inspired to see deeper value in what they are doing. Suppose I offered to pay you twelve dollars an hour to stand in a driving rain and fill large bags with sand. Would you be inspired by that offer?" asked Fred.

"Not really."

"I didn't think so. Let me see if your response changes if I reframe the question. Suppose I told you that your brother's home near the coast was being threatened by an oncoming tropical storm. The only way to stop the rising flood waters and save his home is to create a levee out of sandbags. He has called on his friends and family to help. Now would you be willing to fill sandbags in a driving rain?"

"Well, if you put it that way, of course I would. I'd be willing to fill sandbags for days, if necessary, and there's no way I would take a dime," Dusty said passionately.

"That's what I suspected. Money could not motivate you enough to move you to action. But the thought of helping your brother save his home made you willing to work tirelessly because it was a cause that aligned with what you highly value. The actual work didn't change. In fact, it was exactly the same. But your *perception* of the work changed dramatically. Your paradigm shifted. That is the power of reframing how one views work. You weren't inspired to trade your time for money. But you were passionate and willing to work hard when you knew your efforts would be beneficial to someone you cared about. One of a leader's greatest responsibilities is to shift the emphasis of work from *making a dollar* to *making a difference* in the lives of others."

Dusty's eyes lit up.

"One of my favorite quotes is by Jim Collins, the author of *Good to Great*. He said, 'True greatness comes in direct proportion to passionate pursuit of a purpose beyond money.' Is that what you mean when you talk about living on purpose?" Dusty asked.

"Most definitely! You are living both on purpose and with purpose. You don't just have a mission—you're on a mission. Life becomes intentional and meaningful because you are in pursuit of a calling higher than merely monetary rewards. For-profit companies do well when they operate with a philanthropic passion. Companies become remarkable when they are characterized by a deep desire to make the world a better place. In doing so, they create value for everyone. And making the world better taps into the passion of your people," Fred said as he drew a triangle on another napkin.

"Reframing one's situation to inspire passion is only one side of a triangle. With strong values serving as the base and passion on one side, the other side involves leveraging your individual strengths to create maximum value."

Fred began to write on each side of the triangle.

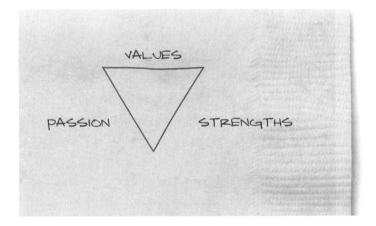

"A lot has been written about discovering and applying a person's talents or strengths. The idea is that exponential results come not by focusing on improving your weaknesses but by leveraging your strengths. On this point, I could not agree more. Far too much time and energy are wasted in performance reviews on 'gap development'—the politically correct way of saying 'weaknesses.' Oh, sometimes we call them 'opportunities for improvement,' but the reality is that investing large amounts of time and energy here rarely pays rich dividends. Focusing on weaknesses keeps the spotlight on self. Focusing on strengths keeps the emphasis on how to bring value to others.

"I'm not suggesting that people resist opportunities to develop new competencies. Certain standards may need to be met to fulfill a given role or responsibility. If left unaddressed, an underdeveloped skill set might cripple opportunities for advancement. Everyone can be encouraged to learn and grow and to expand their knowledge and skills. But what I'm suggesting is that there are certain things you do naturally to near perfection with very little effort. Those are your strengths and should be maximized.

Focusing on weaknesses keeps the spotlight on self. Focusing on strengths keeps the emphasis on how to bring value to others.

"Some aspects of work deplete your energy levels and others elevate them. For maximum productivity, you should seek to do more of the things that energize you and less of the things that drain you. When you are operating in your strengths, you might say that you're 'in the zone.' You experience maximum results with minimal effort. You are invigorated. Time flies and you are confident and empowered when you are operating within your strengths."

"But how do you keep an emphasis on passion and strengths without pushing it to the edge of the slippery slope of entitlement?" Dusty asked.

"Ah, that's a great question," Fred said. "Completing the maxim will address your concern. The most important element is found in the closing phrase of the Maxim of Sustainability. You have to apply your passion and strengths *to solve problems.* Here is where the rubber meets the road.

Passion and strengths are superfluous if not applied to create value by producing effective solutions. Resolving a problem is about bringing something to the table that hasn't been part of the equation before. Tackling tough issues allows us to effectively apply our passion and strengths. And the value created is directly proportionate to the size of the problem resolved. The bigger the problem, the greater the value in its resolution. The bigger the problem, the greater the fulfillment and satisfaction that come from solving it. The key is to look for the largest problem you can find and take it on, applying your strengths and passion to fix it.

"Unfortunately, this is where so many people miss their greatest opportunities. What usually happens when a problem arises in the work setting? What do most employees do when challenged with a tough situation or a project gone awry?" Fred asked.

"They run the other way—if not physically, then certainly emotionally. They want to distance themselves from the problem and pass the responsibility for fixing it to someone else," Dusty answered. A tone of frustration marked his response.

Dusty thought back to the meeting with the task force and the merry-go-round conversation with Ann Marie. No one wanted to assume responsibility for their failed efforts or be held accountable for finding corrective measures. It seemed that most everyone was largely concerned about remaining untainted by any fallout. Finger-pointing and blame-shifting were both employed as several team members attempted to posture and protect themselves. What they really needed was all hands on deck to procure a course of action that would right their listing vessel. Instead, it seemed as if many were strategically lowering lifeboats into the water to rescue themselves.

"That's how most people react," Fred continued. "But the payoff is in creating the greatest value—valucentricity. And what better opportunity than when things are most challenging? If you're only interested in extracting value and preserving an image, then this is risky business. But if you want to make a genuine difference, then the next problem you encounter may very well be your chance. Look to give rather than to get. In a word—*serve*. The more you serve, the more value you create. The more value you create, the more invaluable you become to the organization and to others." Fred once again took his pen and wrote beneath the point of the triangle.

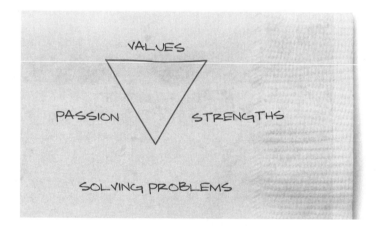

"I'm familiar with the whole concept of servant leadership," Dusty interjected. "But this really brings it into focus. You're suggesting that serving is about creating value for and not simply seeking to extract value from every relationship, encounter, and endeavor. And the best way to sustain value creation is to engage people by making sure their personal values align with corporate values. Then you empower them to solve problems at the intersection of their passion and strengths. When you do that, you not only elevate productivity but also cultivate a culture of positivity. Right?"

"Yep!"

"So how in the heck *do* you do that?" Dusty asked quizzically.

10

Choice

"Elementary, my dear Watson," Fred replied playfully. "You give them a choice."

"What do you mean?"

"A long time ago, a trusted mentor of mine gave me a bit of sage advice. He told me, 'Nothing of long-lasting, positive value ever happens by force.' That's why domination and manipulation never work. You may be able to force your will on others for a season, but you will ultimately fail. As soon as they get out from under your control, they will make their own choices. And typically, the more coercion is applied, the less cooperation is experienced. It may look like cooperation on the surface, but it is usually nothing more than concession or compliance. Either way, the person feels little ownership or passion. I don't care if you're dealing with parenting issues, international political issues, interpersonal issues with a colleague, or corporate issues, people push back when they feel someone is pressuring them. Ultimately, they will make a personal choice. It is the last great freedom."

Fred's last comment reminded Dusty of a quote he'd read in *Man's Search for Meaning*, written by Viktor Frankl. Jim Mitchell had encouraged Dusty to read the book as part of a leadership development program at Query. Frankl was an Austrian neurologist and psychiatrist, as well as a Holocaust survivor. After spending years in a concentration camp and having everything stripped away by his oppressors, he later wrote, "Everything can be taken from a man but one thing; the last of the human freedoms—to choose one's attitude in any given set of circumstances, to choose one's own way." That quote *Nothing of long-lasting, positive value ever happens by force.* had been indelibly ingrained in Dusty's mind. He had always wondered how someone could endure such atrocities and still maintain any semblance of sanity, let alone civility. Now he was beginning to understand—that, too, was a choice.

"Do you remember when we talked about the fact that we've all been given the privilege and responsibility of choice?"

"Yes," Dusty said, opening his manila file folder and taking out the napkin on which Fred had scribbled the clutch situation and growth spiral.

"Well, like we talked about previously, every clutch situation presents a choice—an either/or choice. In every situation, you can either create value or extract value. As you probably remember, a clutch situation is any encounter that requires two or more parties to engage in order to make progress. To engage effectively, everyone's interests must be considered. If you choose to create value, then you will naturally adopt a *we* mentality. You will seek to do what's best for all involved. A *me* mentality, however, short-circuits any attempt to create valucentricity. So in opting to create value, you are choosing to place *we* over *me*. This allows you to evaluate the options and determine which one has the greatest potential to produce the best long-term outcomes for both parties. In other words, it sets you up for a win-win outcome. It sounds like solid common sense to always put *we* over *me*, but the choice to create value is not always so easily made.

"Unfortunately, our natural tendency is to extract value from most situations. By default, humans are self-centered. Children don't have to be taught how to be selfish; they master that all by themselves. When asked to share with another child, they can quickly and clearly express their rights of possession in a single word—*mine*! They have to be taught through example how to share with others. As they grow older, the world reinforces that possessive attitude by teaching them to look out for number one and to ask in a thousand subtle ways, 'What's in it for me?' But the moment someone chooses to extract value, they automatically put *I* over *us*. And doing so creates an atmosphere that can range from mildly competitive to downright antagonistic. This choice to extract value and select one's self-interest over the interest of others ultimately leads to alienation and even desperation."

"But you can't always have a win-win outcome when you are competing in the marketplace. Isn't competition itself a good thing? Doesn't it make us take our game to the next level? How could that be bad? Isn't capitalism itself driven by competitive markets?" Dusty asked, a bit perplexed.

"Competition is great when you are playing games where the stakes are usually inconsequential. We play for the fun of the sport. But life isn't a game. You don't play life! If your winning means that someone else loses, then there can be devastating consequences relationally. It's not that competition itself is bad. Rather, it's the attitude and perspective that someone brings to the experience that make all the difference.

"A perspective that says 'I must win at all costs' is a *scarcity mentality*. If I believe there are limited resources in the world and that to survive I must deprive someone else of those resources, then I will compete to extract value in each situation to ensure my survival. If, however, I possess an *abundance mentality*, then I come at life from a totally different vantage point. In that case, I believe creating value produces an abundance of resources that may be shared by those involved in the creative process. Those who create value are rewarded. They are able to enjoy the value of what they have created through their efforts. And relationships are enriched in the process. An abundance mentality actually dictates that everyone handle resources responsibly for the greater good of all.

"Let me give you an example. My accountant, whom I've trusted for years, recently sold his practice and moved on to other fulfilling endeavors. I had to find another accountant to handle the books for Classic Car Care. After making our selection, I sat down to 'negotiate' a deal with one particular CPA. After clarifying the responsibilities and expectations, I asked her what she would charge for her services. When she told me, I'm sure she expected me to counter by suggesting a lower fee. Instead, I think my response sent her into shock.

"I told her I thought she was worth every penny, and we would be happy to pay her that amount. You should have seen the look on her face. It must have been the first time anyone had ever said that to her. She had no idea what to say. She was loaded and cocked with a comeback to the counter that I didn't offer. After a lengthy silence, she just smiled and shook my hand. Why do you think I did that?" Fred asked Dusty.

"I suppose because you really liked her," Dusty offered.

"Well, I do think her accounting skills are superior, but that's not the reason. Suppose I had tried to hire her for the least amount possible. What if I had hammered her in a negotiation process? What kind of climate would that have established for our relationship moving forward?"

"It might have set her a bit on her heels, but you already said she was expecting you to negotiate her fees."

"Exactly," said Fred. "So how do you think she felt when I did the unexpected—offered to pay her asking rate and told her I wanted us to be 'trusted partners,' both committing to bring as much value to the table as possible for each other?"

"By her reaction, I would say she was obviously surprised. She probably left feeling encouraged and committed to offering you her very best service. Chances are when others are competing for her time and attention, she will probably do everything within her power to make sure you are the first priority," Dusty offered.

"I have every confidence that she will do just that! If I had tried to make her lower her fees, she likely would have looked for ways to hedge or cut services. She may have even resented not making as much money as she could have by working with other clients.

"By expressing my confidence in her and treating her as a valued partner, do you think she is motivated to be fully engaged with a *we* mentality and encouraged to create as much value for us as possible?"

"Absolutely!" Dusty said. "I get that, but you still haven't addressed the issue of competition in a free market economy."

"Thanks for bringing me back to that, because the question of competition is an important aspect of value creation. Competition in the marketplace is not only good—it's necessary. But the perspective you bring to all competitive endeavors is critical: Are you competing *for* or competing *against* something or someone?

"I played football in high school and wanted to be the starting quarterback. I had a good friend who was competing for the same position. One day after practice we went to a local burger joint to talk and scarf down some sodas and chili cheese fries. During that conversation, we came to an understanding that safeguarded our friendship and inspired our play on the field. We agreed that we were not competing *against* each another. Instead, we were competing *with* each other and *for* our team. We made a commitment to bring our best effort to practice every single day so we would push each other to get better. And then we would allow the coaches to decide which one of us they felt could bring the most value to the team in each game situation. By making that commitment, we both elevated our play for our own good and for the good of the team."

"So who was chosen as the starting quarterback?" Dusty asked.

"It's funny you should ask. I suppose I received more playing time, but there was something greater at play than who took the first snap. You see, there were many times when he was tapped to lead the team when I got hurt or when his skills better matched the game situation. We literally worked in tandem. The best part was that he was my biggest fan and I was his. When I was leading the offense, he was watching the defense. Each time I came off the field, he encouraged me and shared his perspective. He not only wanted me to play well but also gave me his best insight to ensure the team's victory. I'll never forget his humility. He put the team's interest before his own and inspired me to play my best. To this day, we are still fast friends. And I aspire to live by his example daily.

"I carried the lessons he taught me into the marketplace and was careful to make it clear to my senior leadership team that we were never to focus on comparing ourselves to other companies in our space. Doing so results in only two possible outcomes. If you compare yourself to others and see yourself as better, then you fall prey to pride. Conversely, if you come up short in the comparison, then you struggle with feelings of inferiority. Both views rob you of the perspective necessary to be your very best. Rather than defining success by comparing our work and outcomes to the accomplishments of others, we strove to pursue personal excellence. In this pursuit of excellence, we were comparing our performance and ourselves to our capabilities. We were intent on actualizing our potential through the creation of value.

"I also made it clear to our leaders that we would never view ourselves as competing *against* other companies in an attempt to put them out of business. Instead, our focus was on competing *for* the customer. Our objective was to create as much value for the customer as we possibly could in both product offerings and service. By doing so, we were competing with others to bring as much value to the market as possible, and we would let the customer decide who had the most to offer. That perspective helped us seize collaborative opportunities *with* others in our space and form strategic alliances that created synergy and brought exponential returns. Many of those opportunities would have been missed had we adopted an antagonistic mind-set of competing against others.

"Whenever we did go toe-to-toe with others in our space, we tried to do so with humility so as to challenge everyone to create as much value for the customer as possible. Ultimately, the market decides who brings the most value. In the process, all players are challenged to elevate their games, and the customer becomes the beneficiary of everyone's best efforts. Those who don't create value are eliminated. That is the essence of competitive markets," Fred concluded.

Dusty had never heard such a clear and concise explanation of competition in the marketplace, nor had he ever thought about competing *for* the customer's best interests. He began to think about all the initiatives across the course of his career that had encouraged competition between business units. Each initiative involved teams competing against one another in an attempt to improve performance. Little consideration was given to how driving the numbers in this way would ultimately impact the customer experience. Now Dusty realized the foolishness of it all. What they had actually done was create silos and establish unspoken game rules that impeded the sharing of best practices. After all, why would one team share their secrets with another team against whom they were competing? Instead, they should have rewarded those people and teams that were sharing best practices and inspiring others to create value for each customer.

"So," Dusty summarized, "in each clutch situation, you have to decide whether you are going to extract value or create value. In doing so, you either put *I* over *us* in an attempt to posture yourself to extract value. Or you place *we* over *me* as you evaluate how you are going to create value for everyone involved."

"Correct," Fred affirmed. "If a person chooses to work with a mind-set of extracting value, then a downward spiral is set in motion that will eventually lead to desperation. Let me show you how that happens."

Fred took the napkin from Dusty, flipped it over, and began to scribble. "If someone places *I* over *us*, then that person has chosen the path of value extraction, which is multiplied by the ER Factor.

$$\text{VALUE EXTRACTION} = \frac{1}{US} \times ER$$

"The ER Factor is about competing against others and positioning self over others—the opposite of humility. ER stands for two components that are always prominent in value extraction: *ego* and *rivalry*. A person's ego leads one to elevate self over others by posturing oneself as smart-*ER*, fast-*ER*, strong-*ER*, bright-*ER*, wealthi-*ER*, and pretti-*ER*, which means essentially bett-*ER* than others. This creates a competitive atmosphere where there is a clear winn-*ER* and a clear los-*ER*. The rivalry has begun. This rivalry introduces another even more crippling element—pow-*ER*. Where there is opposition, the winn-*ER* is usually loud-*ER* and demonstrates more pow-*ER* than others involved. This 'powering up,' or escalation, is the antithesis of collaboration and involves self-promotion and dominance."

"All right," Dusty interjected. "But isn't it sometimes necessary to exercise power in order to move things forward?"

"Great question!" Fred responded. "Don't confuse power with influence. Leadership is about influence—inspiring people toward positive action. Power is about dominance—pushing others to action against their will. And remember the truism, 'Nothing of long-lasting, positive value ever happens by force.' Influence, however, comes by modeling humility and living in growth gear. Living in growth gear, as we said, involves engaging with truth through honest evaluation and maintaining a solution-oriented perspective. Demonstrating a willingness to change for the better inspires others to do the same.

"Those on the ER side of the situation demonstrate no real interest in personal growth. There is no vision for transforming the situation into something for the greater good of all. Rather, defensiveness takes over and individuals resort to *rationalization* to justify their actions and attitudes. When people begin to rationalize behavior rather than facing it honestly and seeking to grow, *stagnation* is the result. Stagnation occurs when there is no solution-oriented perspective. This then impedes collaboration and any movement toward a positive resolution. After a while, people begin to pull away from one another. This *alienation* creates an environment often characterized by *desperation*—where a lack of trust forces people to act in self-protective ways. It is the exact opposite of what is created when people are in growth gear and an atmosphere of inspiration prevails. Choosing to extract value and placing *I* over *us* is always compounded by ego and rivalry. You may get others to agree with you as you rationalize your behavior, but a positive outcome is all but impossible. No matter how many people may agree with you, the reality remains that bad choices have bad outcomes. Bad choices always have a 'gotcha!' And adopting a posture of value extraction is a bad choice."

Fred paused for a moment and then summarized the downward spiral.

"Rather than getting into growth gear through honest evaluation, rationalization disengages the gears of growth. It is the antithesis of authenticity. Rather than facing reality, a person makes excuses and justifies poor behavior. This inability to look at one's self honestly and subsequent lack of ownership will eventually lead to stagnation. As the situation degenerates, a lack of engagement prevents people from relating effectively or connecting deeply with one another. The emotional barriers erected through rationalization to protect our egos are the same barriers that prevent us from authentically connecting with others.

"This emotional distance causes alienation from those with whom we need to connect in order to create value and positive movement. Alienation fosters desperation. People begin to act out of self-interest rather than seeking what is mutually beneficial. Immaturity, rather than growth, prevails.

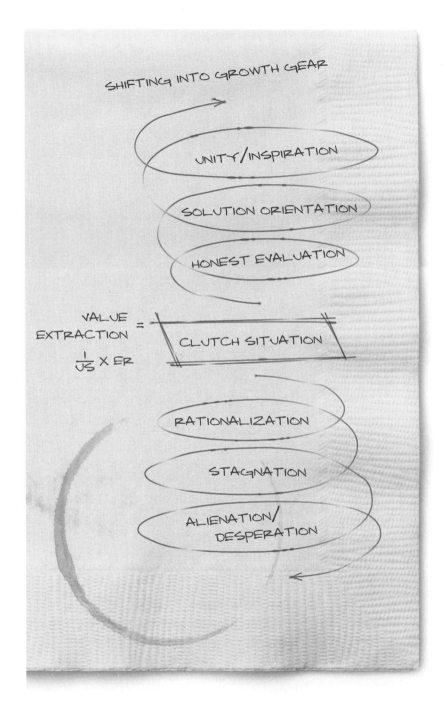

And it all begins with a choice to either create value or extract value. We have to consciously fight our selfish, instinctive tendency to extract value. We must remember in every clutch situation that bad choices always lead to bad endings. Always! Bad choices make bad situations worse—maybe not immediately, but ultimately! Remember, 'Whatever is down in your well will eventually come up in your bucket.'"

Fred sat quietly for a moment and let Dusty process everything he had said. Dusty stared at the napkin and thought through the progression. He had experienced the downward spiral in both his personal and professional life. He could have given multiple examples to illustrate each of Fred's points. Yet opposition was stirring within his spirit, and he had to verbalize it.

"Let me press back for just a minute. Earlier you mentioned parenting issues. How would all of this relate to parenting? Do you believe children should be given a choice? After all, a parent's role is to guide and direct their children's choices until they can become responsible for their own choices. Children don't have a frame of reference by which to guide their decisions."

"That's a great observation. The primary role of a parent is to help a child grow to maturity. Part of that process is learning to make good judgments, which result in good choices. Parents should give their children as many opportunities to make choices as they possibly can so that the choices themselves become a learning experience. Take, for example, eating vegetables—something few children like to do. Should the parent allow the child to choose not to eat them, even though they know how important it is for the child's health? Obviously not! But the parent can still allow the child to make a choice once they have properly framed the options. Since refusing to eat them is not a healthy option, the choice changes. What if the parent were to say something like, 'Johnny, vegetables are important for your growth and development. We want you to grow to be strong and healthy, so you get to choose which two vegetables you want to eat tonight. You don't have to eat a lot, but you do have to eat at least one serving of each. Then, if you are still hungry, you can choose to have seconds of whichever dish you wish. So which two vegetables would you like?'

"The key," Fred continued, "is to offer a reasonable choice without allowing it to become a power struggle. You are the parent. You are clearly in charge, but you want to allow Johnny to make his own choices so he can learn from each outcome and grow to make responsible decisions."

"Sure, but what if it does become a battle of the wills and little Johnny simply refuses to eat vegetables—period?"

"Then you offer him another choice," Fred responded. "He can either choose to eat his dinner—including vegetables—with the family, or he can choose to go to his room alone without dinner. That way you aren't forcing him to eat vegetables. You are simply allowing him to make choices with some very clear consequences. He only has to choose the latter option once or twice, and pretty soon he will figure out that going to bed hungry is far worse than holding his nose while eating a little squash. But the choice is his and so are the consequences. He learns in the process."

"But isn't that cruel and unusual punishment? Sending your child to bed hungry is pretty harsh," Dusty objected.

"Sometimes the choices we have to make in life *are* tough. Life would be pretty easy if our choices were limited to merely good versus bad or easy versus hard. The reality is that most of our choices in life come in the context of much more complicated valuation processes. Many choices present a conflict of values. And every choice we make in life has consequences. Sometimes making the right choice and taking the necessary action needed to create the most value isn't always easy to swallow. But the alternative produces an outcome that is even less palatable.

"There are times, of course, when you have to give directives and can't afford to offer a choice. If someone demonstrates a lack of maturity to make responsible decisions in critical situations, then you are forced to become more direct in your guidance of that person. When the stakes are too high to take a chance on the outcome, then choices become limited. Let's say Johnny chases a ball into the street without stopping to look both ways for cars. That is no time to offer choices. In your loudest voice, you immediately bark a command in an authoritative tone that is unmistakable. There is no conversation or option—you expect immediate obedience! But most situations are not life and death. More often than not, looking for ways to offer choices will enhance the emotional buy-in of the other party."

This whole conversation about force and choice was resonating with Dusty. He was ready to ask for some personal advice. "Well, Lisa and I have a seventeen-year-old son, Mike. We're really having a tough time with him right now. He's a good kid, but he's been copping an attitude recently. He is bright and talented but not motivated to do his best work. To be blunt, he's lazy and a bit rebellious. I have to bug him a lot to get him to pull things together. After all, he will be applying to colleges soon, and he has to get all of his ducks in a row if he wants to get into a good school. How would this all apply to Mike? If I'm not direct in guiding him and firm in my demands, then I'm afraid he'll slack off and squander his future."

"What college does he want to attend?" Fred asked.

"We've visited five campuses but haven't made any decisions. Right now the plan is to apply to all five and see what responses we get."

"Great plan, but that wasn't the question. What school does *he* want to attend?"

"We want him to get into a school with a good MBA program. That way when he finishes his studies, he will be set for a nice future in business," Dusty offered.

"I'm not asking what you want. I'm asking what Mike wants. You see, herein lies the dilemma. What you want for Mike may not be what Mike wants for himself. If Mike wants it, he will work for it. If, however, he feels like he's only living out your dreams for him, then he has no opportunity to demonstrate mastery over his own thoughts and feelings. He needs the freedom to pursue his own dream. He may conform for a season, but sooner or later he will become resentful and rebel against what he feels is your power to control his destiny. The reality is that your dream for him and his dream for himself may be one and the same, but he needs to make that decision for himself. Only then will he be fully engaged and motivated.

"Have you ever wondered why so many college freshmen literally throw away a semester or an entire year of school by skipping classes or generally goofing off? Could it be that while they were at home so many decisions were made for them that they never learned to become responsible decision-makers?

Or maybe they were forced to pursue courses of study at schools they were never genuinely interested in attending in the first place. Consequently, they didn't feel they had ownership of the choice or of their own lives because Mom and Dad were so heavily involved in the decision-making processes. Throwing away a good opportunity could be an expression of rebellion against a decision they felt they weren't allowed to make for themselves. They never really *owned* the decision and therefore never made an emotional investment in the outcome. They were neither encouraged nor equipped to live on purpose.

"Rather than telling Mike what he should want to do, why don't you help him set up some choices? Then let him decide. Eventually, Mike will begin to make responsible choices to reach his own goals. Help him think through the options objectively without interjecting too much direct guidance, unless he asks for your input. Here's a great axiom to remember anytime you feel the urge to express your opinion: *Unsolicited advice is rarely well received.* So instead of telling him what to do, help him frame the options. Then express your confidence in his ability to make good decisions and wait for him to ask for your counsel. If he asks, great! If he doesn't, that's all right too. He has to own his decision.

Unsolicited advice is rarely well received.

"Making a decision of this magnitude is certainly important, but it's not the end-all of choices. If he chooses poorly, then he can always transfer later to another school. And if his course of study proves to be unfulfilling, he can always change majors down the road. The point is that he is far more likely to take responsibility for the decisions he makes for himself. If you make the decision for him and it falls apart, then he could always blame and resent you for it. That doesn't mean you don't have high hopes and standards or you don't hold him accountable. Express your deep belief in him and encourage him to fulfill his potential. But remember, growth cannot be attained through force and manipulation. Mike has to fully own his decision and the resulting consequences. Owning the decision and taking responsibility for his actions are what we call maturity—or living on purpose."

11

Responsibility

"Any discussion of maturity brings us to the fourth and final maxim. The Maxim of Responsibility states that ownership empowers people to take responsibility for creating value," Fred explained. "Being value-centric means that in each and every clutch situation, you make choices you believe will generate the greatest value for everyone involved. Then you wholly own those decisions and act responsibly by taking the necessary action to create that value. In essence, you take ownership and responsibility for your choices. Again, it's an eithER/OR decision. In this case, OR is an acronym for *ownership* and *relationship*. Ownership means that an individual assumes responsibility for their decisions and actions, while relationship implies a desire to stay engaged with others to create healthy interpersonal connections. An emphasis on OR leads to a strong decision-making capability. OR is the only path to empowerment.

"Let me ask you, Dusty, who has more vested interest in any business venture, the owner or the person he has hired to be the manager?"

"Obviously the owner!"

"So who is more likely to act responsibly and expend discretionary effort to make that business successful?"

"The owner."

"Right!" Fred responded. "Ownership carries a deeper sense of personal responsibility. In the same way, many people talk about the need for adding value, but few are willing to take ownership and assume responsibility for creating the value they say they want. Even when people understand the power of these principles, they have to consciously choose to create value, or they will be prone to follow their natural inclination toward a more selfish approach. What I'm saying is that so much of this is counterintuitive. You see the tension each time a problem surfaces. Those who 'own' value creation jump in the fray and tackle tough issues. Those who prefer to 'manage' the situation tend to distance themselves from anything that might disrupt the status quo.

....

The Maxim of Responsibility

Ownership empowers people to take responsibility for creating value.

....

"For any company, a primary consideration should always be, 'How do we structure our organization to allow everyone to think and act like owners?' When people feel they 'own' the business, or at least a part of it, they also feel responsible for guarding its activities, resources, and relationships. Simply stated, where there is a sense of ownership, there is deeper emotional attachment. Ownership empowers people to take responsibility for creating value, thereby enhancing results."

Dusty thought for a moment about various members on his team and how some of them tended to respond when things drifted sideways or blew up altogether. Meetings meant to address the question of responsibility for poor outcomes were often met with crickets. In an attempt to avoid responsibility and possible rejection, everyone sat back and waited for someone else to make the first move. Nobody was willing to step up. He wondered how much more productive they could have been had someone assumed ownership of the situation rather than looking for ways to pass the buck. He mused for a moment about what might have been accomplished had his team members wholeheartedly applied their passions and strengths to solve problems rather than emotionally distancing themselves and deflecting issues onto others.

"Sorry," Dusty said, realizing his attention had strayed. "I got lost in my thoughts for a moment. I definitely see how this plays out in real life. There is a stark contrast between ER and OR, isn't there?"

"Absolutely," Fred responded. "When you shift your thinking and put the emphasis on OR, it changes everything. Taking ownership for your actions and seeking to strengthen relationships in everything you do make a world of difference. The emphasis shifts to doing what's right and what will bring the most value to life. It becomes less about *comparison* and more about *contribution*. It becomes less about *competition* and more about *collaboration*. And it is where you find fulfillment. It creates the ultimate win-win-win in each situation. Movements of good always begin with OR—ownership and relationships."

"In other words, eithER one will seek to protect and promote oneself and extract value from each situation, OR they will make choices to seek to serve others by bringing value to each situation," Dusty interrupted. "If someone seeks to extract value, then they place *I* over *us* and everything becomes focused on ER. However, if a person seeks to create value, then they place *we* over *me* and move forward with an attitude of OR, taking ownership of their choices and strengthening relationships. Essentially, OR multiplies your efforts to create value by plugging you into the power of valucentricity."

Fred smiled as he wrote on another napkin.

$$VC = \frac{WE}{ME} \times OR$$

$$\frac{2}{1} = 200\%$$

"Now watch the power of this idea," Fred continued, with passion in his voice. "In this formula, VC obviously stands for value creation. Watch what happens when *we* is placed over *me*—you essentially get 2 over 1, or a total value of 200%. Now let's suppose you have a team of 4 people. When you place the good of the 4 and the contribution of the 4 over the 1, you get a total value of 400%. The Value Creation Equation shows the power of multiplication. When leaders learn to empower their people and employ these principles, they leverage the power of multiplied effort and increase productivity exponentially. Valucentricity is generated. You can see how powerful this quickly becomes. When all contributors apply the OR Factor, substantial movements of good can be created.

$$VE = \frac{1}{us} \times ER$$

$$\frac{1}{5} = 20\%$$

"On the other side of every clutch situation is VE or the Value Extraction Equation. By placing *I* over *us*, you essentially get 1 over 2 or 1/2. If the team in consideration is larger, then the results are diminished proportionately. So if you have 5 team members who are all seeking to extract value for themselves, then you essentially have 1 over 5, or 20 percent of the potential performance of their combined efforts. On the VE side, people are divided and so is your effort. Essentially, you are unplugged from the power of valucentricity. Performance on the VC side is exponentially increased, while performance on the VE side diminishes rapidly," Fred concluded.

"So value creation multiplies your efforts, while value extraction divides both performance and people."

"Well said," Fred said. "When you apply these formulas to teams, the negative and positive impacts can be stunning.

Take an example from the world of sports. Do you remember the US men's basketball team at the 2004 Summer Olympics?" asked Fred.

"Of course," replied Dusty. "The team was stacked with a bunch of young, talented players like Dwyane Wade, Carmelo Anthony, and LeBron James. Then you had two recent MVPs in Tim Duncan and Allen Iverson to round out the roster with what should have been another Dream Team."

"Right, but what happened?"

"They blew up. They literally imploded. They couldn't get their act together and play as a team. By all outward appearances, some of the players were more interested in making a name for themselves than in representing something larger—like the team or even the United States. It was embarrassing. They expected gold and barely walked away with the bronze medal. As a team, they were certainly divided and their efforts were diluted."

"No doubt about it! Now, do you remember the US ice hockey team at the 1980 Winter Olympics?" Fred asked.

"Sure! When they beat the team from the Soviet Union, it was dubbed the 'Miracle on Ice.'"

"You know your sports," Fred said. "Up to that point, the Soviets had won nearly every world championship and Olympic tournament since 1954. *Sports Illustrated* touted the US team victory as the top sports moment in the twentieth century. An inspirational and unconventional coach named Herb Brooks led them to defy the odds. But here is a telling question: How many players can you name from that team?"

Dusty thought for a moment. No names readily came to mind. "I don't think I can name any of the players. I was pretty young in 1980," Dusty said in his defense.

"Of course you were. But isn't it interesting that you cannot name a single player from a match that was deemed the top sports moment in the twentieth century? That's because it wasn't about individual players. It wasn't about egos and spotlights. By his own assessment, Brooks was more interested in getting the right players than he was in getting the best players. When he brought them together, he challenged them to be bold and to play for something greater than themselves. He focused all their energy and effort on playing for one another and the country. And he inspired them to greatness. Together they created a national legacy that will long be remembered.

EithER the culture will alienate teammates and divide and dilute effort, OR it will unify a team and multiply effort.

"Every team or organization has a culture," he continued. "Culture is nothing more than the collective expression of the values, beliefs, and behaviors that individuals bring to the endeavor. EithER the culture will alienate teammates and divide and dilute effort, OR it will unify a team and multiply effort. You can have a culture by design or by default—either way, culture is paramount. A culture of value creation and multiplication is inspirational. A culture marked by alienation and division is usually characterized by desperation."

Dusty once again sat in silence, allowing the force of the formulas and their outcomes to solidify in his mind. It was becoming increasingly clear to him just how impactful this information could be on both a personal and a professional level. Finally, Dusty uttered, "Wow, this really is powerful stuff!"

12

The Question

"Let me remind you," Fred said, "that assuming owner-ship and making good choices aren't always as easy as they sound. We've all been conditioned to one degree or another to protect and provide for ourselves first. This myopic, me-first mentality flies in the face of value creation and makes valucentricity virtually impossible.

"To effectively confront this mentality, there are two issues to consider. First, you must focus on bringing the greatest value to everyone whom the decision may impact. Such a decision-making process is others-focused. It's all about the *we*. There's a quote by Sir John Templeton that brings this into perspective. He said, 'Never forget, the secret to creat-ing wealth for oneself is to create it for others.' We benefit most by bringing value to others. Also, we must focus on long-term value generation versus the immediate benefits of any decision."

Dusty understood exactly what Fred was talking about. The sting of their earlier conversation about Mike had unmasked the fact that he was acting more in his own self-interest than in Mike's interest. He knew that, all too often, he had attached his own self-worth as a parent to Mike's performance. Pushing Mike to excel said more about his own insecurity than it said about his son. Dusty had come to realize through his conversation with Fred that he had not modeled for his son what it meant to live on purpose. Though he had good intentions, his own self-protective and self-promoting tendencies were skewing his ability to create real value for one of the most precious people in his life. Dusty knew that many of his instinctive reactions were creating no value. Quite the contrary, they were often relationally destructive. His need for control, which was an attempt to protect both his heart and his image, had caused strain in almost every close relationship in his life, including in his relationships with Mike and Lisa.

"Never forget, the secret to creating wealth for oneself is to create it for others."

Sir John Templeton

"So how does someone stay focused on creating value?" Dusty asked.

"That, my friend, leads to the most impactful question," Fred responded. "In becoming a champion of value creation and coaching others to do the same, I have found it helpful to keep a guiding question front and center in my thinking. Every time I encounter a clutch situation, I always ask myself the Clutch Question." Fred turned the napkin over and scribbled these words on the backside:

THE CLUTCH QUESTION:

WHAT'S THE SUPERIOR CHOICE?

"The superior choice is always the one that creates the greatest value. If I consciously ask myself this question in every situation, then I can hold my knee-jerk reactions at bay and make better decisions. The key is to pause and consider the options. Whether I'm facing an important decision, engaged in a conversation, or involved in a potentially volatile situation, I can act intentionally and live on purpose. Rather than being reactive, I can respond in a manner that is consistent with my values. I can consciously make proactive choices that have a much better chance of creating valucentricity.

"Let me give you two real-life examples," Fred continued. "Let's say I want to lose a few pounds. I know I will need to exercise regularly and watch what I eat. It's all about calorie intake and burn, right? So I start regularly working out three days a week, walking, and lifting weights. Now with every meal, I have a choice to make. Either I choose to eat foods that will sabotage my efforts, or I make good choices that will create the greatest value. When I make poor food choices, I am minimizing the gains that I could be making through exercising regularly and eating healthy. As simple as that sounds, I'm amazed at how many people will rationalize a poor choice by labeling it a 'reward,' when the real reward of achieving greater value is being sabotaged. Will I justify poor choices or synergize my efforts with good choices? Rationalize or synergize—it's a choice.

"When I choose to live on purpose, I opt to live healthily. When I make the decision to be healthy, many of my choices become crystal clear. The decision to be healthy impacts my food choices, my workout schedule, my sleep, and my overall self-care. My values are aligned, producing valucentricity on a personal level.

"Another example is how we respond to others in the heat of the moment. Although Anne and I have been married for more than forty years, she would be the first to tell you that we have been *happily married* for somewhat less than forty years. How much less depends on the mood she is in when you ask her," Fred said with his usual grin.

"That's because I have not always applied the OR Factor in our marriage. Whenever Anne and I have a 'spirited discussion,' which is what I prefer to call a fight, I often allow my self-protective reactions to overtake my conscious processes. As a result, I react in some very unpleasant ways. Consequently, I've spent more nights in the guest room than I care to admit. Through practice, I've learned—admittedly, all too slowly—how to stop myself from reverting back to old patterns of communication. Whenever the conversation turns 'spirited,' I ask myself the Clutch Question: What's the superior choice? Then I can take ownership of my choices and make the relationship my higher priority. I've found that when I apply the OR Factor in my business or personal life, it really works. Rather than being reactive to the situation, I become proactive by making choices that produce the greatest value. I engage in the process of evaluation to seek a solution that can lead to an inspirational conclusion—both of us wanting to be better."

While Fred talked, Dusty's mind wandered to the many uncomfortable encounters he had experienced with Lisa. When she'd express even the slightest disappointment in him, he would immediately become extremely defensive. Why did he instinctively behave like that? Did he have a deep-seated need to manage his image or protect his tender ego? Why did he deflect responsibility rather than take ownership of anything that might reflect poorly on him? He could now clearly see how he had often lived out the downward spiral, making matters worse. It always frustrated Dusty how the smallest issues frequently turned into verbal knock-down, drag-out fights. Conversations quickly turned into arguments, leaving the two of them shouting from opposite sides of the room. At times, they could hardly stand to be in each other's presence. He certainly wasn't thinking of creating value in those clutch situations.

He was more interested in maximizing Lisa's faults and minimizing his own. Now he saw that approach as nothing more than a feeble attempt to rationalize his behavior. Rather than making the superior choice to create value, he often turned the conversation around to cast a shadow of blame on Lisa, which only alienated her and created a more desperate situation. He wondered how very different things might have been in each of those scenarios if he had simply asked himself the Clutch Question and made a superior choice to create value.

"Are you all right?" Fred asked.

"Oh, I'm fine. It's just that this all hits a little too close to home—no pun intended. I was just thinking of myriad situations with Lisa in which I failed to create value. I'm afraid I have really blown it," Dusty humbly admitted.

"Yes, you have!" Fred said with a sarcastic tone. "And so has everyone else on the planet. One thing I learned a long time ago is that the more personal you think something to be, the more universal it actually is. Dusty, we've all blown it. That's why this is so profound. The only way to reverse the damage is by changing the pattern of behavior by applying these principles of value creation and making superior choices," Fred said.

He let the thought hang in the air.

After a long pause, Fred continued. "In simply stopping to ask the Clutch Question, a progression takes place. The mental process of making superior choices begins with *consideration*—slowing down long enough to stop oneself from reacting and taking time to consider the possibilities. This prevents a knee-jerk reaction. I can literally stop myself from reacting and being driven by self-protective behaviors. The ancient word *sider*, which is where we get the word *consider*, literally means *wisdom*. When I stop to consider the options and their possible consequences, I am thinking wisely.

"The next step in the process is valuation, or evaluation—the weighing of those options. I want to give significance or weight to each option according to my value system—what I deem to be most important. By doing this, I place greater value on one thing over another. At this point, I am pondering which decision will lead to the greatest long-term value.

Then I commit to the best option and take action. Actions speak louder than intentions. Actions speak louder than goals. Actions are the only true reflection of commitment. Your actions, not your words, reveal the true condition of your heart and mind."

"Or you could say, 'Whatever is down in your well will eventually come up in your bucket!'" Dusty said playfully.

"Well said. It's all about making the superior choice. By taking ownership of the choice and focusing on what's best for the relationship, we are plugging into the power of valucentricity.

"The second element we must think about is long-term value. Each time we make a decision, there is a short-term and a long-term dimension to consider. Too often people make decisions based only on the short-term outcomes. Many decisions have a short-term gain but carry a long-term loss, while others have a short-term loss but ensure a long-term gain. When faced with the choice, far too many people opt for the short-term benefit and forfeit the potential to create greater value in the long run.

> *"Whatever is down in your well will eventually come up in your bucket!"*

"Here's an example from my own life. Anne and I just moved into a garden home. With the kids grown and gone from the home, we didn't need the big house anymore. So we sold it and moved into something smaller. I have the time and enjoy being outdoors, so I decided to do the yard work myself. The problem was that I had no equipment. I picked up a nice used lawnmower at a garage sale, but I needed an edger. I went to the local home and garden store and started investigating the options. In addition to the basic tools, they had some really cool, top-of-the-line, high-powered stuff with all the bells and whistles.

"As I was drooling over the equipment, a young sales associate approached and asked if he could help me. He could tell right away that I was a pushover. I was practically selling myself on the most expensive edger in the line. He could have agreed with me and sold me that edger, but he didn't. Instead, he asked why I needed an edger. When I explained that my yard was extremely small and my needs were meager, he suggested two other options at much lower price points. He was down-selling me on an affordable option that fully met my needs. He could have sold me the more expensive edger and benefited in the short-term. However, if I got home and experienced buyer's remorse over having purchased something I really didn't need, he could very likely have had a disgruntled customer who might never return to the store.

Many decisions have a short-term gain but carry a long-term loss, while others have a short-term loss but ensure a long-term gain.

"Fortunately, I came to my senses and realized he was right. I could have easily paid four times the price for something I never would have needed. But he chose to create the greatest value for me, the customer. He actually took a short-term loss—a lesser sale than he could have made. But in doing so, he received a long-term gain—he made me a customer for life. He gained my trust and loyalty. Now every time I return to that store I ask for that same sales associate. I would dare say I have spent a small fortune on home repairs with him serving as my advisor.

"Now let's apply that same thought to my relationship with Anne. If she comes at me aggressively during one of our lively conversations, I could choose the short-term benefit of defending and justifying my actions. In that moment, it may feel good and appropriate to prove myself right, but in the long term, it could cost me much more than my short-lived satisfaction. However, it may feel like death in the short run to adopt a humble attitude and ask her to show me my shortcomings. But in the long term, that kind of humility lets her know that I'm placing *we* above *me* and that I want to learn how to create as much value as possible for *us* in our relationship."

Fred took a deep breath and gave Dusty time to think. Dusty looked at the napkin with the Clutch Question written on it. He couldn't believe that such a small piece of recycled paper could contain so much wisdom. *What's the superior choice?* If he could truly understand and apply that simple question, he knew it could radically change his personal life and the way he conducted business—for good.

Dusty thanked Fred for his time, and the two men parted company. Dusty had a lot to do to prepare his presentation for the Employee Engagement Task Force. Ideas about how to craft an approach that would create the greatest value for Query's customers and team members flooded his head. All day Friday and throughout the weekend, Dusty pored over his notes and researched.

He crafted a deployment proposal that included a series of workshops, each designed to teach team members the maxims of value creation. He decided to follow up these workshops with a series of short, high-impact online coaching videos designed to reinforce the principles taught in the workshops. He thought this form of "drip development" would be well received since it didn't require team members to go offline for long periods of time. A steady stream of video segments would expose them to transformational content in bite-size coaching editions they could easily apply. It was all coming together.

By midday on Monday, Dusty was ready to make his presentation to the task force. That night he was like a kid before Christmas. He couldn't remember when he had been so excited about a presentation's potential outcome. He could hardly sleep as he kept imagining the flow of the meeting the following morning. The funny thing was that his excitement had less to do with his presentation and more to do with what he imagined could be the start of a corporate cultural transformation. If everyone understood and applied the principles of value creation, then it could be truly revolutionary. The night was short but restful.

Dusty was anxious to get to work the next morning. He actually noticed that he had a genuine spring in his step and a brighter attitude as he walked into the office. He could hardly wait to see what opportunities the day would present. And he knew that in every clutch situation he would be asking himself, "What superior choice will produce valucentricity?"

PART 4

ADVANCEMENT

Happiness pursued, eludes; happiness given, returns.
SIR JOHN TEMPLETON

13

Transformation

As the task force members started to gather, Dusty looked out the windows of the conference room on the sixteenth floor. The panoramic view of the city was breathtaking. A storm had gathered clouds over the city and was threatening to bring heavy rains. But on the horizon, the morning sun was breaking through the heavy clouds and throwing beams of light to the ground in a stunning display. Dusty used this amazing visual as a metaphor to begin the meeting.

"According to the data, less than one-third of the American workforce could be described as 'actively engaged,' meaning that they bring enthusiasm, passion, and creativity to the work experience. More than half of the workforce is 'not engaged,' with about 20 percent being 'actively disengaged.' According to many experts, the figure for lost productivity due to a nonengaged workforce is estimated to be around $640 billion a year in the United States alone. This lack of emotional attachment to work leads to low morale, lack of loyalty, sparse innovation, and less-than-stellar performance. Though this dark cloud threatens to rain on our efforts, I believe we have the opportunity and the resources necessary to shine a light as bright and beautiful as the one you can see on the horizon," Dusty said as he pointed out the window. *The introduction was providential*, he thought to himself. Not a bad way to start the meeting.

Then he set up the conversation about value creation by showing them a formula he had come across in his reading. He felt it vividly illustrated the issues at play. Dusty wrote the formula on the white board:

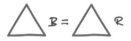

"The deltas represent change," Dusty said. "If you want to change the results that you are getting, then you have to change the behaviors that produce those results. Many people might call this behavior modification. If company B wants to get the same results as company A, then it may analyze and attempt to emulate the same policies, procedures, and processes company A employs. The problem, however, is that company B rarely produces the same results. This is because a specific way of thinking drives company A and causes employees to act in a certain way. Those smart enough to recognize this reality may pursue a wide array of training initiatives to reframe the way people think about their environment and how they process information. This is what psychologists would call cognitive therapy. It is an attempt to help people see life and activities from a different and hopefully more productive vantage point. And, as such, it can positively impact behavior and ultimately productivity.

$$\triangle \xrightarrow{T} \triangle B = \triangle R$$

"If you really want to create long-lasting, positive change, then you have to know what drives the thinking behind the behaviors, which produce the results. That element, which is foundational to both our thinking and our behavior, is our value system. Values create the grid through which our thoughts, decision-making processes, and performance are all integrated. So if you want to change the results, then you have to assess and align the values, which give rise to the thinking, which produces the behavior that garners the results. In effect, this is the formula for cultural transformation. When people's values are aligned, thinking is refined, inspiring synergistic behavior and elevated performance. When people feel inspired to perform at a higher level, they achieve superior results.

$$V_A \rightarrow \triangle \xrightarrow{T} \triangle B = \triangle R$$

"What we need to do to reach our full potential is allow our values to drive our business. We need to define, articulate, and embody our values. We need to select team members whose values align with the values embraced and embodied by others within the organization. And we need to reinforce the principles of value creation in everything we do."

Dusty paused for a moment to look at everyone's body language. He wanted to make sure that everyone was engaged. And from what he could sense, he definitely had their attention.

But before he could continue the presentation, Dan, a key influencer on the team, pointedly asked a couple of questions. "So how do you judge whether or not someone has strong values? Couldn't it get rather dicey if we begin to claim that we can accurately assess someone's morals or character?"

"Let me clarify," Dusty responded. "When I say 'values,' I'm referring to how people evaluate certain aspects of the world around them. Values are shaped by how much importance an individual places on certain elements in a decision-making process. This way of viewing certain dimensions of life and work has as much to do with functionality and productivity as it does with ethics and morality.

"For instance, if I were to ask you if you value safety, I'm sure you would answer with a resounding yes. If I were to ask you if speed and efficiency are important, you would also likely respond in the affirmative. But what happens if I place you in a situation in which it is impossible to complete a task on schedule while also taking the time necessary to adhere to the safety procedures? Which gets the short end of the stick? Do you complete the task on time, while demonstrating risky behavior? Or do you place safety above meeting the deadline? Either way, you have just made a decision based on what you value more. Neither choice speaks to your morality. Such a process of evaluation has more to do with effectiveness than with ethics, but it deals with your values nonetheless. Your decision shows clearly whether safety or timeliness is more highly valued.

"The problem is that many companies do not clarify what is of greater importance. They say both are vital and leave it up to the individual to make a determination. In doing so, the organization sets everyone up for frustration. There will always be those who will choose to err on the side of timeliness and others who will choose to err on the side of safety. This creates confusion. Without clarity, anyone can find themselves wedged between a rock and a hard place, unable to get unstuck because they are being pulled in two opposing directions.

"But suppose that same organization takes a firm stand to value safety over speed. That is not to say it disregards the importance of deadlines, but it makes it clear that if the employee must ever choose one over the other, then they should always choose safety first. Now it is clear where the company stands. When it comes to the issue of safety, they can live it, hire to it, teach it, and reinforce it to make sure everyone is on the same page. In essence, leadership can assess and align the organization around safety as a key value. They can begin to build a culture around safety. There is no confusion in regard to this issue. It is clear—safety first!

"Now suppose that within that same culture, individuals choose to skirt safety procedures for the sake of efficiency. They may very well be good, moral people with a strong work ethic, but they are risk-takers who are willing to forgo certain procedures in order to get more work done. What do you do with those otherwise productive folks? If you let them continue without intervention, you jeopardize your reputation as a safe company, and other team members will begin to question whether or not the company truly values safety. Assessment and alignment are the key. Workers must be groomed to understand that when safety and timeliness conflict, safety must come first. With that clearly established, people choose either to adopt safety as the superior value or find themselves in direct conflict with the organizational culture. When there is no clear value alignment, the organization is reduced to a police state where leadership enforces adherence to certain behaviors. When alignment is strong, unity, harmony, and productivity prevail. Alignment produces valucentricity—the flow of energy that comes through synergy."

Dusty could tell that what he was saying resonated with the team. A few people even nodded their heads in agreement, so he continued.

"Value adoption cannot be forced. Values are always chosen on a personal level. It is a fact that nothing of long-lasting, positive value ever happens by force. Forced compliance never leads to healthy collaboration. Instead, it creates a warped culture. Where values are misaligned, you have a culture by default rather than by design. But when a group decides collectively what is highly valued and alignment is strong across the organization, remarkable movements of good result."

Dusty took a deep breath and remained silent for a moment to let his words sink in. Then he summarized his thoughts before opening the floor for discussion.

"The most powerful competitive advantage for any organization is a compelling culture. Culture is really nothing more than the composite of the values, beliefs, and behaviors of the individuals who comprise the organization. Culture, then, is the collective expression of individual values. Companies do not possess values—people do. Crafting a values statement and hanging it prominently in the lobby is nothing more than an aspirational activity if the people in the organization do not embody those values. But when the people's values align with the organization's direction and commitment, a culture is crafted where people are free to express their passion, use their gifts, and fulfill their potential in creating value. In essence, taking action to assess and align values can positively impact an organization's culture. Rather than being aspirational, aligned values can become transformational.

"A strong culture makes it possible to create movements of good, which become the superior organizational advantage. A culture that creates movements of good will be characterized by trust and unity. In this superior culture, synergy replaces silos. Competition is minimized and collaboration becomes the norm. And, last but not least, individual self-promotion is marginalized in the shadow of collective value creation and celebration. A company's culture is the engine that generates the power to drive movements of good. A healthy corporate culture will create value for everyone.

A strong culture makes it possible to create movements of good, which become the superior organizational advantage.

"Having everyone on the same page fosters a Remarkable! culture where people believe the best *in* one another, want the best *for* one another, and expect the best *from* one another."

Having framed the conversation, Dusty and Jim co-led the rest of the meeting. Dusty presented the maxims of value creation and explained what it means to live on purpose. There was healthy discussion, and nearly everyone was fully engaged in the process. Ideas were bouncing around the room like popcorn heated in an open container. The meeting was scheduled to last until noon, but it was so productive that everyone agreed to clear their afternoon calendars and have lunch brought in.

The team was captivated by the maxims and how they might apply them to impact performance in positive ways. The concept of empowerment was not new to anyone, but the succinct manner in which Dusty so clearly articulated and applied it was refreshing. Dusty couldn't remember a time when there had been so little conflict and so much collaboration in a meeting of leaders. Even when impassioned challenges or penetrating questions arose, Dusty was less defensive when addressing them and relied on the Clutch Question to center his thinking on value creation. It was one of the most productive meetings he had ever experienced at Query—or in his career for that matter. Time literally flew. Finally, late in the afternoon, Jim brought the meeting to a close.

As the meeting concluded, Jim approached Dusty. With a smile as wide as the Mississippi River, he patted Dusty on the back and simply said, "Well done!"

Dusty knew in that moment he had begun a process that had the potential to bring great value to the organization. Collectively, they had the opportunity to create a movement of good like none they had ever seen. He knew it would be a process and wouldn't happen overnight. But he was excited about what the future could hold for him and his teams as they sought to create value for their clients, one another, and ultimately for the company. He was energized, optimistic, and hopeful. His passion had been renewed.

Cultural Transformation Formula

$$V_A \rightarrow \triangle \quad T \rightarrow \triangle \quad B = \triangle \quad R$$

When people's values are aligned, thinking is refined, inspiring synergistic behavior and elevated performance. When people feel inspired to perform at a higher level, they acheive superior results.

14

Resistance

Dusty and Fred met weekly while Query was in the early stages of what the leadership team called the VC Initiative, with its accompanying workshops and "drip development." For the most part, employees responded to the developmental work with rave reviews. However, there were pockets of resistance and a few negative voices that frankly caught Dusty by surprise. He knew that any initiative would be met with some measure of resistance, but the feedback from the few was still disheartening. Being the recovering perfectionist and control freak that he was, the negativity of the naysayers began to get under his skin. Like termites embedded in the load-bearing beams of a house, they began to eat away at the core of Dusty's confidence in what the team was attempting to build. He worried that the presence of such negativity might stifle the group's ability to create the kind of culture he was beginning to dream was possible.

A particularly painful encounter came when one of his direct reports and team leads named Lanny blindsided him with some feedback on the initiative. Dusty had always maintained an open-door policy, only closing his door when he needed privacy or didn't want to be distracted. Late one afternoon, Lanny knocked on the open door of his office.

"Come on in, Lanny. What can I do to create value for you this afternoon?" Dusty asked.

"Dusty, I just need to talk. I don't know that I'm fully on board with all of this value creation stuff. I mean, I don't understand exactly what I'm supposed to be asking my people to do. There are few metrics to monitor progress and no objective standards to which I can hold my people accountable. I'm having a hard time wrapping my head around how I'm expected to lead my team in this initiative if there aren't specific goals we are driving."

Dusty understood why Lanny was having such a tough time. After all, it was difficult to create a checklist that, when completed, was guaranteed to produce value. Furthermore, how could value creation be objectively measured anyway?

Lanny had a military background and had risen to the rank of colonel before retiring from the service and entering the private sector. He was a respected leader and top performer who had been tapped to oversee a floundering operations team. He had taken a lackluster, undisciplined team and turned it around by applying additional metrics and timetables to monitor progress. Every goal was broken down into objectives, and every objective had action items with deadlines. The results exceeded the company's expectations. By all accounts, Lanny was a gentle giant. But it was clear that he equated top performance with strict adherence to rigid guidelines with little room for personal expression.

Lanny's team was productive, but Dusty always felt they lacked passion. The cubicle landscape of Lanny's team looked like a barracks at boot camp. Every desk was clutter-free. People kept very few personal items at their workspace, and corkboards were filled with graphs and charts. The overall tone throughout the space was almost somber. Collegial conversation was noticeably absent. Everyone actively participated in "the drill," but there was very little camaraderie. When five o'clock rolled around each day, it appeared as if everyone had gone AWOL in his unit. *If any team needed to understand and apply the maxims of value creation, it was Lanny's team*, Dusty thought to himself.

Lanny was all about driving business. He was a true tactician. And it wasn't that he lacked genuine concern for his team members. It was more that he felt someone's personal life should never interfere with their professional performance. He believed firmly that you have your personal life on the one hand and your professional life on the other—and the two should never meet. Therefore, he never attempted to get to know what his team members' lives were like outside the office. They really didn't know much about his either—and he liked it that way. There was a secure, nonemotional, neutral zone between the home and the office. It made his work as a leader much more objective, or so he thought.

"Dusty," he continued, "all of this emphasis on positivity is a bit too touchy-feely for me. How do you hold someone accountable for creating value? It's all too philosophical and fluffy. As for all this talk about passion and leveraging strengths, what does that have to do with business? My team is only as strong as its weakest link. Everyone in my charge had better be proficient in all aspects of the work, or I'm a poor leader. If a single team member isn't armed and on guard, then the entire team's productivity could be compromised. That is why I work so hard to cross-train and regularly assess each team member to make sure there are no glaring deficiencies."

"Lanny, there is no doubt in anyone's mind that you've done a stellar job meeting your business objectives. Your team has exceeded just about every metric that's been put in place to drive productivity. But do you ever wonder if your people really enjoy their work?"

"May I be direct?" Lanny asked.

"Of course you can," responded Dusty.

"Dusty, frankly, it's not about enjoyment. The way I see it, if my team members are receiving a paycheck twice a month from this organization, then they had certainly better be 'engaged' in their work," Lanny said as he made quotation marks in the air with his fingers. "It's not about personal satisfaction—it's about fulfilling their duty. I agree with the principle of taking responsibility for your actions. It's the responsible thing to do the work you are paid to do—period!"

Dusty admired Lanny's work ethic. He had turned around a floundering team by establishing drills and discipline. But he certainly would not describe Lanny's team as flourishing— even though their numbers were impressive. He wondered how long many of them would stay with the organization if given an opportunity to go elsewhere.

"Lanny, let me ask the same question another way. Imagine for a moment that you had no corporately bestowed authority, no title, and no officially appointed position.

What if you had no ability to remunerate or reprimand the members of your team? Imagine that you had nothing but your values and a mission. How many of the people in your charge would show up tomorrow simply because they believe in Query's mission and in you as a leader? How many possess a deep sense of purpose and passion for what they do? In other words, are they emotionally invested in the work?"

Lanny sat silently. The expression on his face reflected his bewilderment. Dusty continued to drive the point.

"Don't you serve on the board of the Rescue Mission?" Dusty asked.

"Yes, for almost five years now."

"Picture that group, or any one of a number of nonprofit organizations. They all do good work and have committed volunteers. Those volunteers give their time and energy without receiving any payment. Why? It's because they believe in the cause. They are aligned with the organization's values and vision. What they receive in return for their work is a greater motivator than money. They are led by passion and purpose. Of course, we are a for-profit organization. We do have the ability to reprimand and remunerate. But I often wonder how much more innovative and productive we could be if our people possessed that same kind of passion for their work.

"Lanny, I deeply believe that kind of passion has everything to do with an employee's ability to live on purpose and create value. The more our values are in alignment as a team, the more value we can create for everyone. Unity is a powerful force in driving productivity. And I am asking you to throw your influence into this initiative. Even if it doesn't all make sense to you right now, will you at least agree that the two of us can keep talking it through?"

Lanny took a moment to reflect without responding. Then with measured words he finally spoke. "Dusty, I'll commit to keeping an open mind and a conversation going with you. But I will be candid, and I will not mince words. You won't have to guess where I stand. If I begin to feel that this is all bunk, then you will know it."

The more our values are in alignment as a team, the more value we can create for everyone. Unity is a powerful force in driving productivity.

"That's all I can ask right now," Dusty responded. "But don't wait for me to approach you. If there is something on your mind that you want to talk about, you know where to find me. Let's keep the conversation going about how we can make this change practical and meaningful."

As Dusty watched Lanny leave the office, he couldn't help but wonder where this situation was going to lead. He knew the organization was on the right path. He also knew each team member would have to make a personal choice to follow that path. Dusty had come to understand that choices were a vital part of the maturation process. Each time he began to feel the angst rise within him, he fought off the tendency to power up and issue directives. Rather than resort to his normal reactive ways, he would remind himself that "nothing of long-lasting, positive value ever happens by force."

15

Remarkable!

Thursday afternoon when they met at the coffee shop, Dusty skipped the cordial small talk and immediately started firing questions at Fred.

"So how do you handle resistance? What do you do when people drag their feet and challenge the basic premises of value creation? And, more importantly, how do you hold people accountable while attempting to create this kind of cultural transformation?"

"Those are great questions! Which leg of the skunk do you want to pull first?" Fred responded calmly with a deadpan look on his face.

"Let's talk about dealing with resistance first," Dusty said. "It drives me crazy when people attempt to sink ideas or initiatives before they ever give them a chance to float. In the break room at work, we have a framed picture of a sailing vessel with a caption underneath that reads, 'In order to discover new worlds, you have to lose sight of the shore.' It's an obvious encouragement to be bold and courageous. But too many people are simply cowards when it comes to change. We'll never get out of the port if people start blowing holes in the bottom of the boat before it ever gets into deep water. The irony of it all is that the hole punchers are actually *on the boat*. As long as we're bailing water while we're in shallow water, we're never going to discover new worlds. How do you deal with those who want to swamp the boat before it gets out of the bay?" Dusty asked with a distinct tone of agitation.

"Why does opposition surprise you, Dusty? This isn't your first voyage. You know there will always be some measure of resistance to change. Some people struggle with it more than others. You will always have early adopters and those who are cynical and resistant."

"You're right, but I'm surprised by some of the people who just don't seem to get it. What do you do with people who choose to be negative?"

"In your question, you have your answer," Fred said.

"What do you mean?" asked Dusty.

"You said, 'people who choose to be negative.' They're making a choice. They're choosing to live in the shadows rather than enjoy the sun. And every choice has consequences. Dusty, let me be blunt and cut to the chase. There are three types of people who will rapidly deplete the energy of any organization. Those types of people are the *victims*, the *naysayers*, and the *know-it-alls*."

Fred paused to take a long, slow drink from his cup of raspberry tea. He savored the blend for a moment as if to draw additional strength before engaging in a draining conversation. Then he continued.

"Victims view problems as personal persecution rather than impersonal challenges to overcome. They walk through life waiting for the anvil to fall. They're often angry, usually annoyed, and almost always complaining about having been taken advantage of by someone. For them, the world is not safe and people cannot be trusted. Victims see problems in every opportunity. They look for and attract others who feel they have been treated unjustly. Ultimately, victims are self-destructive. They live out negative self-fulfilling prophesies that are deeply rooted in their own sense of unworthiness. Don't get me wrong. Occasionally, we all see ourselves as victims, but chronic victims have chosen to turn their negative view of the world into a way of life. The saddest part is that they often seem to enjoy playing the role of the victim. That's probably because they can evoke sympathy from others by recounting their sad stories. That is, until they begin to drain the lifeblood out of everyone around them. They are emotional black holes, sucking the positive energy out of everything and everyone they touch."

"I know the type," Dusty chimed in. "At first, you want to help. But after a while, you begin to realize that life for them is a nonstop series of crises. What about the naysayers?"

"Naysayers are perpetually pessimistic. Nothing is ever good enough. Nothing will ever work. Nothing you or anyone else can do will ever get them to see the brighter possibilities in life. Naysayers are the Eeyores of life. You remember Eeyore, the character from Winnie-the-Pooh? He's the old, gray donkey who mopes around, speaking monotone and casting a negative pall over everything. He lives in the southeast corner of the Hundred Acre Wood, in an area labeled 'Eeyore's Gloomy Place.' He lives in a stick house, which collapses quite often. He thinks poorly of most of the other animals in the forest. And, of course, Eeyore's favorite food is thistles, which speaks volumes.

"Naysayers block progress. They may claim to be realists, but they are not. A realist sees a situation for what it is but can still be vibrantly optimistic. Naysayers, however, tend to highlight the negatives and doubt the possibilities. They use the darker crayons in the box to color life and generally can be characterized as gloomy, pessimistic, and depressing. Naysayers are fools who cannot be convinced that there is any other way to see the world. Dark lenses cloud their worldview. They are momentum killers and a cancer to any organization."

"And," Dusty interjected, "just like the victims, naysayers end up fulfilling their own negative prophecies. It's sort of like what Henry Ford said: 'Whether you think you can, or you think you can't, you're right.' Because they think negatively, for them, it cannot be done."

"Right," Fred said. "But here is a kicker—despite their negativity, naysayers can be hard workers. The problem, however, is that for all of their work, they create very little true value. Their identity is often defined by what they are against. On the surface, they may give the impression of having a strong work ethic. They may possess passion and pursue a cause with intensity. But you have to understand what drives them. Naysayers are fighters. As long as you align with their view of reality, they can be fierce defenders. But the minute you oppose them, they can turn on you and fight against you with the same intensity they have demonstrated toward other 'enemies.'"

Dusty began to think of people along his career path who epitomized what Fred had just characterized as a naysayer. He remembered vividly debates during which he had attempted to convince a naysayer of the value of a project. He recalled how frustrated and exhausted he had felt after those nonproductive point/counterpoint conversations. He could count a number of times when a naysayer had deadlocked a conversation, initiative, or project until the stalemate eventually had to be broken with an edict.

Even then, the grumblers might hold out in the deployment phase. They may concede and comply but exert very little discretionary effort to guarantee the work's success. *They have no concept of the OR Factor*, Dusty thought.

"And then we have the know-it-alls," Fred said with a deep sigh. "A know-it-all is smarter than everyone else on the team, at least in their own mind. You may have heard it said that 'leaders are learners.' Well, a know-it-all can never be a true leader. In their own estimation, they have little left to learn. They're the expert on everything. They purport to be a leader, but very few follow. When they walk out of the room, others roll their eyes. They cannot engender trust because they lack humility. A know-it-all is constantly trying to position themselves as the go-to person who has all the answers. The interesting thing is that if you watch closely, rarely does anyone turn to them. Nonetheless, they'll offer their opinion on just about any topic anyway. Do you remember when I told you that unsolicited advice is rarely welcomed? Well, the know-it-all hasn't figured that out yet."

By this point, Dusty was a full sponge. He had absorbed so much that he was beginning to leak. With each description, he envisioned team members who were guilty on all counts. He could no longer contain his frustration. "So what am I supposed to do? I can't just waltz into the office on Monday morning and start doling out reprimands and pink slips. And besides, how have these folks been able to fly under the radar for so long?"

"Let's take those questions in reverse order," Fred suggested. "Could it be that the reason you haven't noticed these behaviors until now is because you have created what I call a *directive culture*? Your work environment tends to lend itself toward a leadership model that doesn't allow for much freedom of expression or creativity or innovation. In other words, very little discretion is needed or allowed. Decisions are all dictated for team members. As a result, there is little true ownership. People are going through the motions to hit the numbers and fill in the blanks. But that's about it.

"But now you're talking about living on purpose and encouraging people to use their passion and strengths in new and creative ways to maximize productivity. You're allowing them to make their own choices, which is the only way you can get discretionary effort. But the flip side is that when they make those choices, they may actually reveal their true dispositions for the first time. What may have been suppressed in a more mandated environment begins to surface as you pursue more purposeful value creation."

"That makes sense," Dusty offered, "but what is the appropriate response when you identify these negative behaviors?"

"Do you remember our conversation about the youngster who wasn't keen on eating his vegetables and how we framed the choices for him?"

"Yes."

"Well, you frame the conversation with your team members in much the same way. First, you explain why certain behaviors are important: 'It's necessary to eat vegetables if you want to grow to be healthy.' In your case, clarify that you are crafting a culture in which you expect everyone to generate valucentricity. And in order to achieve such a cultural shift, living on purpose must be the rule.

"Next, you frame the choice in such a way that you express confidence in their ability to make good judgments: 'Which two vegetables would you like to eat?' or for your team, 'How would you accomplish our objectives in the most effective manner while maintaining a positive environment?' Then you let them make the choice. As long as the key performance indicators are being met—eating vegetables with a good attitude—it doesn't really matter which vegetables they choose to eat, because you have offered them only healthy choices. Likewise in business, there are many ways to accomplish the same objective. Allow latitude where you can, without compromising the outcomes. Let them own the choice and be responsible for the results.

"If they blatantly refuse to pursue value creation and positivity or seek to negotiate unreasonably outside of the parameters, then you offer them another choice—one with well-stated consequences. Either they can buck against the established values and thereby choose to move in a different direction vocationally, or they can take ownership and act in ways that support the organizational objectives and strengthen relationships. Again, the choice is theirs, and the options have been clearly delineated."

"So you're establishing your values and making them clear. Then you're allowing everyone the opportunity to choose whether or not they will align their personal values with those of others within the organization. Is that correct?" Dusty asked.

"You've got it," Fred responded. "People will begin to self-select. Of course, your hope is that everyone will choose to align with value creation and become invested in the outcomes. However, that's a bit idealistic. Not everyone will want to sail that ship. You'll quickly be able to identify the victims, naysayers, and know-it-alls. Then you can deal with them appropriately. And deal with them you must. Their presence can be crippling.

"At this point, it's also important to note that leaders must be careful not to label people prematurely or inappropriately. Leaders must first ask themselves profound questions to become self-aware and make sure they are leading well. Remember, honest self-evaluation is necessary to shift into growth gear. Sometimes employees are resistant simply because leaders are leading poorly."

"How is that?" Dusty asked.

"Sometimes leaders move so quickly that they blow right past buy-in and start issuing edicts. I know I've thrown a lot at you. But if you have time, I'd like to give you a formula regarding effecting positive change and getting everyone on board," Fred offered.

"I'm not overloaded yet. I think I can handle one more formula from my mechanic mentor," Dusty responded playfully.

"Good, I'm glad to know you still have a little bandwidth left." Fred reached for a napkin. Notes on napkins had become standard protocol for their meetings.

"In the spirit of *we* over *me*, there is another challenge I often lay before leaders. It has to do with making sure they have broad-based buy-in before they execute their ideas or strategy. If leaders move too quickly toward implementation without adequately garnering support, it can be perceived as a power play and create resistance in the ranks. Let me show you how this all plays out," Fred said as he wrote:

$$Qi \times A = E$$

"In this formula, the Qi stands for *quality idea*. It could be a product, a service, an initiative, or a dream for the future. The A represents the *adoption* of that idea, which is a reflection of how well team members are aligned in their values and thinking. Where values are aligned, high levels of trust and respect exist. This high trust culture oils the gears, which must be engaged to produce movement toward a desired end or objective. The E stands for *execution*, or the effective implementation of that quality idea. If low levels of trust and a lack of alignment mar a company's culture, then adoption is hard to attain even if you have the best ideas in the world. Let me show you how this looks in practice.

"Let's say that another company has a world-class idea for a product. It ranks as a 10 on a scale of 1 to 10. It's really a game-changing concept. However, imagine that the culture of that organization is weak, and leaders are prone to push initiatives through without broad-based buy-in. In that case, we might give them an adoption rating of only 6. That would make their overall execution score a 60 on a scale of 100. But let's say you have a relatively good idea that might be rated an 8. By all objective measures, it is a slightly inferior offering. However, because of high trust, good leadership, shared values, and positivity, the culture of your organization provides an adoption rating of 10. In this scenario, your overall execution score is an impressive 80, which is to say that there is a 20 percent greater likelihood that your idea will be translated into reality and make it to market than that of the other company. That is the power of a healthy culture."

"That makes sense," Dusty offered. "I've seen a lot of great ideas fail simply because people weren't emotionally vested in the process."

"So have I," Fred added. "Sometimes I see leaders who are unwilling to seek advice or allow their ideas to be challenged or refined in the adoption process. They may feel that compromising on the idea gives too much away, so they bulldoze through opposition and push their agendas. What they fail to realize is that the very act of mandating actually diminishes the impact of a quality idea because you build emotional resistance. What might seem to be expeditious is, in reality, impeding the execution. Impatient leadership compromises the strength and momentum that could have been gained through valucentricity—aligning, unifying, and energizing the team.

"You see, the best product doesn't always win in the market. Nor does the brightest employee always rise to the top of the corporate heap. Companies that thrive are resilient, tenacious, and, most important, unified. Creative, innovative, and adaptable also describe Remarkable! organizations. But unity is by far the most powerful force for good, and it's the result of a healthy culture. The best companies know that culture trumps everything else, so they are intentional about crafting engaging and compelling environments. They don't leave culture to chance. It never happens by default. Culture is always by design in companies that are making a significant difference. Values are defined and aligned to cultivate an inspirational culture. Does that make sense?" Fred asked.

> *Unity is by far the most powerful force for good, and it's the result of a healthy culture.*

"It makes perfectly good sense," said Dusty. "The impact of culture in any organization cannot be overstated. I can see now that culture is the single most important factor in the success of any organization and must be leadership's highest priority. A company's culture is its greatest competitive advantage, and it will either multiply a company's efforts or divide both its performance and its people."

> *A company's culture is its greatest competitive advantage, and it will either multiply a company's efforts or divide both its performance and its people.*

"Correct," Fred responded. "The most important issue facing any business is to intentionally craft a Remarkable! culture of value creation. Everything else is secondary."

"You are going to have a culture," Dusty interjected. "The issue is whether your culture will be by design or by default. Will intentional value creation be the force that crystallizes your culture? Or will you lean toward value extraction by default. And will it be conspicuously unusual, delivering

> *The most important issue facing any business is to intentionally craft a* Remarkable! *culture of value creation.*

products and services that exceed all expectations? If you deliver extraordinary value, then people will talk about you. And when they talk about you, indeed you have become Remarkable!"

"Stated with clarity and confidence," Fred affirmed. "In the process, valucentricity will serve to elevate engagement and improve morale, garnering discretionary effort from your team members. Now one last thought I want you to consider."

"What's that?"

"The only way to help others learn and apply the maxims of value creation is to embody them yourself. If you want them to impact your family, then it starts with you. If you are trying to transform an organization's culture, then it has to start with you. You have to choose to start the process. You have to take the OR path. You must assume ownership and make relationships your highest priority. Mahatma Gandhi once said, 'Be the change you wish to see in the world.' Change *around* you must always begin *within* you. The superior choice is about taking the initiative to create value."

> *Change* around *you must always begin* within *you. The superior choice is about taking the initiative to create value.*

When Fred mentioned the superior choice, it reminded Dusty of what he had been carrying with him for weeks. He reached into his wallet and retrieved a napkin. He gently unfolded it and placed it on the table in front of them. On the napkin, Dusty had consolidated the growth spiral and

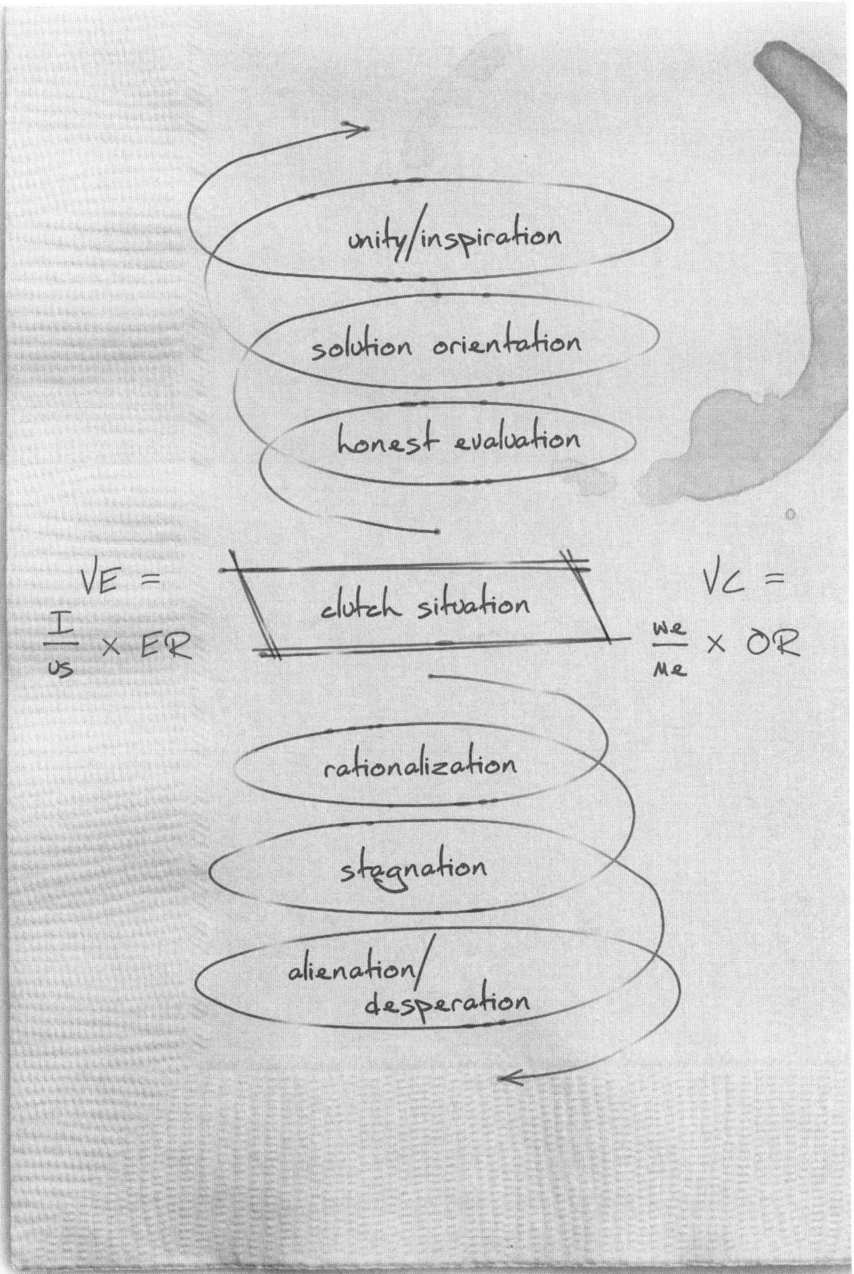

unity/inspiration

solution orientation

honest evaluation

$$V_E = \frac{I}{us} \times ER$$

clutch situation

$$V_C = \frac{we}{me} \times OR$$

rationalization

stagnation

alienation/
desperation

the value creation formula. Fred cracked a wry smile as he looked at the napkin. After a moment, Fred turned the napkin over. On the other side, Dusty had written the Clutch Question. Once again, Fred took a pen from his pressed shirt pocket. He wrote a big *P* in the center of the napkin, just below the question.

"The P," he said, "stands for pivotal point. It is any clutch situation. It is the place where decisions are made that will begin a journey toward either alienation or transformation and unity. At each pivotal point, I can choose to place the emphasis on *us* or on *I*," Fred explained as he wrote them on either side of the P. "If I choose to put *we* over *me*, then I have chosen to emphasize *us* and will seek to create value for *us*. However, if I place *me* over *we*, then I will seek to extract value and make choices that will disengage the growth gear and start a descent down the spiral. Again, it's a choice.

The Clutch Question:
What's the superior choice?

US   P   I

"Living on purpose means that the choice is always in my hands. I have to choose whether I will pursue the ER or the OR path in life. The ER is about ego and rivalry against others—positioning myself to extract value. OR is about taking ownership and highly valuing relationships. Notice that the first person pronoun *I* always stands in the middle of that choice, because I alone can make that decision. I cannot expect others to move first. I must take the initiative in the process of value creation. I must act responsibly in making the superior choice to create value." Fred wrote on the napkin again.

The Clutch Question:
What's the superior choice?

US P ER I OR

Dusty looked for a moment at what Fred had written on the napkin. In a flash of insight, it all came together. Like staring into a hologram and seeing the third dimension pop off the page, he saw the elements of the superior choice all right there before his eyes.

With excitement in his voice, Dusty began to recap what he had heard Fred say. "The P represents the pivotal point, which is any clutch situation. On one side of the P is *us* and on the other is *I*, representing the choice to either create or extract value. The *I* also stands for personal responsibility to choose between either ER or OR. Flip the *us* and bring it all together and you have all the ingredients necessary to make the SUPERIOR choice!"

Dusty took the pen that Fred had placed on the table and wrote on the napkin:

> The Clutch Question:
> What's the superior choice?
>
> US P ER I OR
>
> SUPERIOR

"I really think you've got it," Fred said as he smiled from ear to ear. "You see, you set yourself up to become Remarkable! when you take the time to ask the Clutch Question: What's the superior choice? It forces you to tap into the core of who you are and draw strength from those things you value most. It allows you to act consistently with what you hold in highest regard and prevents you from becoming a prisoner of your self-protective devices and knee-jerk reactions. In other words, you *live on purpose* and act in a way that rises above the circumstances. You actually create value by design while you live intentionally. And when you act in ways that defy what others expect—you seek to continuously create value rather than extract value—people take notice and remark about it. Those remarks invariably create a buzz about you and your business. People will be talking both inside and outside the organization about how conspicuously unusual you are in a marketplace filled with people who are seeking merely to extract value. And when others begin to describe you as extraordinary, then indeed you have become Remarkable!"

16

Reward

In Dusty's reading, he ran across a quote that reminded him of Fred's challenge to always take the initiative in value creation. He had it framed and hung in his office to remind him of where transformation must always begin. A monk wrote it anonymously centuries ago, but Dusty knew its truth was timeless. It reads:

I Wanted to Change the World

When I was a young man, I wanted to change the world.

I found it was difficult to change the world, so I tried to change my nation.

When I found I couldn't change the nation, I began to focus on my town. I couldn't change the town, so as an older man, I tried to change my family.

As an old man, I have come to realize that the only thing I can change is me. Now I understand that if

long ago I had changed myself, I could have made
an impact on my family.
My family and I could have made an impact on
our town. The influence of our town could have
helped shape the nation, and thereby I could have
changed the world.

Change at Query came slowly and steadily at first. The
maxims of value creation became consciously grafted into
the organization's culture. Leaders were constantly challenged to embody them. They guided team meetings. New
associates were encouraged to embrace them. Conversations
throughout the organization were peppered with the language of value creation and positivity. The mission statement
was made ever-present and modified to read:

"Creating Value for Everyone We Encounter"

And it wasn't merely the text of the mission statement that
had changed. Employees at Query no longer simply *had a
mission*. They were *on a mission*. And the difference was Remarkable! One department took the initiative to produce and
distribute wristbands. They were engraved with the words
CREATE VALUE, reminding everyone to stay on the OR side
and shift into growth gear to generate valucentricity. Best
practices, which employees had once hoarded as competitive advantages over other business units, were shared freely.
Friendly competition, which once subtly created silos within
the organization, was replaced by collaboration and colle-
giality. Associates began to voluntarily show up for work a
little earlier during heavy work cycles and stay a little later
when deadlines were approaching.

At the same time, when team members put too much time on the clock, leadership noticed and encouraged them to also spend appropriate time creating value at home with those who mattered most. Organizational health seemed to follow personal health. When people's personal lives were better, they brought a better self to work and productivity increased.

After several months, the metrics moved in a positive direction. It took time for the concepts of value creation to take root, but when they did, they spread like bluebonnets across Texas in spring. Positivity eventually swallowed up negativity. Naysayers, know-it-alls, and victims were either converted or called out.

Dusty knew the company was on the right track. He could sense and see a new spirit emerging. Team members felt empowered as they were encouraged to maximize their passion and strengths to solve problems. Associates were talking about how they could create movements of good for their clients and for one another. A swell of hope and optimism significantly raised the energy level within the office. And customer satisfaction scores improved as advisors dedicated themselves to taking ownership of customer relationships and responsibility for resolving issues completely. Team members were talking openly about how proud they were to be part of Query's vision and mission. At the same time, they were experiencing a significant uptick in referrals. The word often used to describe the change that was taking place was Remarkable! But the changes that most excited Dusty were taking place at home.

Dusty had been making a conscientious effort to be less critical of Mike. He quit offering unsolicited advice and tried hard to curtail his need to control his son's every move.

Instead, Dusty looked for ways to encourage Mike to explore his options, own the decision-making process, and take what he felt was appropriate action. As Dusty exercised less control over Mike's life, Mike began to feel empowered.

As a result, Mike gave more thoughtful consideration to his choices, knowing he alone would have to face the consequences. Although Dusty still felt the need to make it clear that he would not rescue Mike from the outcomes of poor choices, it was an unnecessary warning. Mike began demonstrating maturity and discernment in almost all of his decisions. He started taking more initiative in his schoolwork and completed chores around the house before being asked. What Dusty had interpreted as laziness was nothing more than Mike's way of expressing his frustration over feeling powerless to make his own decisions.

For the first time in a long time, Mike initiated conversations with Dusty and asked for his advice. Rather than pontificating, Dusty learned to ask thoughtful questions, which allowed Mike to come to his own conclusions and then make a choice he could own. Debates were replaced with meaningful discussions about Mike's hopes, dreams, and aspirations. The wall of defensiveness that had been built between them was being dismantled brick by emotional brick. It was happening gradually, but resentment was giving way to mutual respect.

Trust was being restored. After a while, they actually started to enjoy each other's company again. As a result, they worked together to plan trips to two college campuses—schools of Mike's choosing. And, best of all, they both looked forward to spending the time together discussing the options for Mike's future.

The biggest changes, however, were taking place in Dusty's relationship with Lisa. The tone of their interactions immediately began to change when Dusty started applying the principles of value creation and making superior choices in their relationship. For years, he had attempted to get his needs met by extracting value from their relationship rather than seeking to bring value to it. Now his attitude had been radically altered. Rather than demanding or seeking to manipulate Lisa into meeting his needs, he asked questions about how he could enrich their relationship. And he listened intently to her answers.

He tried to anticipate her needs and bring the greatest value to every conversation and situation. He thought and acted in ways that had Lisa's best interest at heart. Rather than finding fault in her, he was more conscious of his own shortcomings. This new self-awareness cultivated within him an attitude of humility. With that humility came a confidence like nothing he had experienced before, because he knew he was leading by example for the first time in their lives together. Rather than being threatened by the knowledge of his weaknesses, he was emboldened to keep himself in growth gear.

Dusty was inspired to invest in his relationship with Lisa in new ways. For years, he had sought to advance his skill set for the sake of advancing his career. Now he was seeking every means possible to advance their marriage. He read books, registered the two of them for a marriage conference, and put a date night on the calendar each week so they could be alone and have meaningful conversations.

At first, Lisa was skeptical of Dusty's intentions and honestly a bit confused. She wondered what aliens had abducted her husband and left this foreign being to replace him.

Though he tried to explain to her all that he had learned about value creation, he was much more effective in doing so at the office than at home. Dusty was often frustrated by her cool response to his enthusiasm, but he tried his best to be patient. Rather than try to explain, he made a personal commitment to live on purpose and lead by example. He was choosing to continue to create value in their relationship regardless of her response.

When Lisa became angry or expressed disappointment, he fought back his natural tendency to rationalize his behavior. Instead, he chose to be open and humble, avoiding the slippery slope toward alienation. He stayed fully engaged in each situation and conversation, evaluating the options and seeking a solution that would inspire them both to become better. And in those moments when he slipped back into old patterns, he was quick to own his actions and apologize before he defaulted into a defensive position, escalating the situation and making matters worse.

To moderate his expectations, Dusty convinced himself that it was going to take quite a while for Lisa to work through the broken trust issues that had built a barrier between them. It would take time to get back to a place where they could once again confide in each other. He had made a commitment to himself that he would strive to demonstrate extraordinary patience during this period of healing. He was surprised, however, by how soon Lisa started to soften once she saw a noticeable change in his attitude and demeanor toward her. It didn't happen overnight, but she slowly began to feel safe in his presence again.

For the first time in a long time, she no longer felt that she had to fight to protect herself. Fear and trepidation gradually yielded to openness and curiosity. Trust was being restored one encounter at a time. She was beginning to feel as if she had found a long-lost friend. A transformation of a personal nature was taking place—one Dusty could have neither orchestrated nor dictated.

As for Dusty, he was content with incremental progress and was actually enjoying the opportunity to court his wife again. He knew they had much to rebuild, and it would be a lifelong process. But that was all right with him, because now he knew that he wanted to spend the rest of his life with Lisa, and he felt confident that he was on the right track. His heart had experienced a cataclysmic shift. He really wanted the marriage to work and was willing to invest whatever time and energy were necessary to woo back the bride of his youth. He was all in. The more he focused on the *we* and creating value, the more he saw Lisa soften. He was confident that with enough time and consistency, Lisa would be able to climb out of her self-protective tower and join him in the process.

Life had changed dramatically for Dusty since Fred first gave him a ride home the night his car's clutch failed. The idea of a clutch had taken on a whole new meaning. Now he saw every interpersonal encounter as a clutch situation—an opportunity to engage with others in a transformational way. He now asked himself the Clutch Question at every pivotal point, which allowed Dusty to make the superior choice and move toward value creation. His decisions were now framed within the context of *we* over *me* thinking, and the OR Factor multiplied his efforts. He began to inspire not only those around him but also himself. Dusty no longer felt helpless and desperate. He no longer felt the need to control those around him. He was in control of himself.

He was growing to be an exemplary leader, and he was enjoying the contentment he felt—both at work and at home. Dusty was empowered by the confidence that his choices could have a positive impact on his corner of the world. Consequently, broken relationships were being restored. Life was marked by less conflict and more unity. He no longer felt the need to compete with others in a feeble attempt to prove his value. Seeking collaboration in every clutch situation opened new worlds of possibilities. For the first time in his life, Dusty felt at peace with himself and the world. He was living for something much bigger than himself. He was living on purpose. And he was experiencing valucentricity. Life was good.

The changes Dusty had experienced since his first conversation with Fred at the coffee shop were Remarkable! His perspective on life had shifted significantly since he had discovered and started applying the maxims of value creation. And he wasn't the only one who was being positively impacted. As he took the initiative and made the choice to create and bring more value to every encounter and endeavor, those closest to him began taking notice.

Dusty knew that if the principles he had learned over the past few months could so profoundly and positively impact his closest relationships, then they would continue to create a better culture at work as well. It was all about making better choices—superior choices—that possess the power to unify a diverse workforce by focusing on value creation and personal responsibility. It seemed so simple, yet it was so profound. By making better choices, Dusty was creating a better life for himself, his family, and Query. He no longer had a problem with his clutch. In fact, Dusty had become a clutch player—standing in the gap and offering peak performance under pressure.

On the work front, the principles of value creation had an unexpected impact. The concept of value engineering had taken on a whole new meaning. Rather than just trying to engineer costs out of their offerings at Query, employees began to look for ways to engineer more client value into each offering. Value was now defined by the experience, not just by the expense. As Query provided more value, clients less frequently questioned the company's pricing structure. As a matter of fact, Query made it abundantly clear that it was not the lowest-cost provider in the space. Employees actually began to take pride in the fact that they no longer used lowballing as a sales strategy, and loss leaders became a notion of the past. Instead, the company offered unexpected value for the price. As a trusted partner, Query was becoming known for delivering extraordinary service that went above and beyond expectations. And as a result, people were beginning to talk about their Remarkable! customer service experiences.

Amid this metamorphosis, Dusty was reaffirmed in his belief that an organization's culture is its only real advantage—the superior advantage—in the marketplace. A truly differentiating culture is characterized by empowerment and value creation. It is a culture in which people are inspired to perform at a higher level. This performance must be the result of synergistic behavior, which happens when values are aligned.

This Remarkable! culture produces an environment in which silos are shattered and synergy prevails. In such a setting, movements of good have the potential to produce exponential returns, reducing competition and amplifying collaboration. Loyalty, morale, and discretionary effort are all increased as by-products of value creation. Cultures in which people believe the best *in* one another, want the best *for* one another, and expect the best *from* one another are conspicuously unusual. When you experience them, you can immediately tell they are different. And people are compelled to remark about them. This kind of culture invariably creates a buzz about your business.

Dusty also understood that creating such a culture—whether in a family or a multinational corporation—begins with a personal choice. And Dusty had committed himself to be intentional about crafting a Remarkable! culture in each corner of his world—one choice at a time. He had discovered the simple truth that in every clutch situation each one of us has a choice to make: we either extract value from or create value for those within our sphere of influence. And when we choose to create value, the results truly can be Remarkable!

17

Renewed

Time flew, as it often does when life is full and efforts are unfettered by the fear and doubt of negativity. Query flourished. Morale soared, and performance reached new heights. Lessons learned from past challenges became coaching fodder for each new wave of team members. Creating value became reflexive, and movements of good quickly gained momentum throughout the company. Valucentricity had become Query's legacy.

But time also took its toll, as it inevitably does, on mortal frames and mechanical parts. Its effects were inescapable. One day on his ride home from work, a young executive noticed the brakes in his car were making a horrific grinding noise as he slowed at each intersection. It was obvious that the pads had worn thin and needed to be replaced.

Being new to the city, he had yet to research auto shops in the area. Between his recent move and his new job, he had neglected some of life's more mundane details. But experience told him that to delay replacing his brake pads could soon become a costly mistake. He remembered hearing his neighbors say good things about a garage conveniently located just a few blocks off of his usual route home. Whenever he had ventured in that direction, he had actually noticed that this particular garage always seemed abuzz with activity.

Having left the office a bit early to enjoy a long weekend, he decided to stop in at the garage to inquire about their services. As he approached the modest building, he recognized the Classic Car Care sign and pulled in. Entering the modest lot, he came to a grinding halt in a parking space reserved for "Friends" and hopped out of his car. As he walked toward the door, a stately middle-aged man with bright blue eyes and a slightly receding hairline approached him. His khakis were soiled but neatly pressed. In addition to the Classic Car Care emblem blazoned across his shirt pocket, he sported a warm and welcoming smile.

"I'm new to the area, and I was hoping you might be able to answer a few questions about your services," the young man said, initiating the conversation.

"Well, I would be delighted. If you'd like, we can go into my office where we can chat over a couple of bottles of cold water. But first, let me introduce myself. My name is Dusty, and I happen to be the proud owner of this fine establishment. It would be my pleasure to explore how we might be able to create some value for you today."

Appendix A

Roadmap to Remarkable!

The following pages are an excerpt from *Roadmap to Remarkable!*, which was created to help individuals and organizations apply the principles found in *Remarkable!*

For more information or to order copies, visit: CreateRemarkable.com/resource or RoadmapToRemarkable.com.

INTERSECTION 4

REMARKABLE CULTURE
CHARTING THE COURSE

def: **Culture**
The collective expression of the values,
beliefs and behaviors that INDIVIDUALS
bring to any endeavor.

Wherever people gather, you have a culture. It's the environment people create when they gather, whether at home, at work or at play. It becomes the defining characteristic of that group. Every individual either strengthens or diminishes that culture.

Culture will "happen" either by default or by design. If you want to create a Remarkable culture, you have to be INTENTIONAL about the journey to get there.

A Remarkable culture is one in which people ...

BELIEVE THE BEST IN EACH OTHER
WANT THE BEST FOR EACH OTHER
EXPECT THE BEST FROM EACH OTHER

Most of us are clear on what we EXPECT FROM the people around us. But have you ever given any thought to what you WANT FOR the people around you? First, you must know them...

- Do you know what makes each of them individually happy or fulfilled?
- Do you know their stories?
- Do you know their hopes, dreams and aspirations?
- Do you know their challenges and limitations?
- Are you creating the kind of environment that allows them to fulfill their dreams and flourish, using their strengths and passion?

GETTING TRACTION: Identify 2 or 3 things you can do to improve the culture of each of your environments.

REMARKABLE! CULTURE SURVEY

Read each statement below and provide the score that most accurately reflects your beliefs regarding the organization in the space provided to the left. Rank your responses on a scale from 1 to 10, with 1 = strongly disagree; 10 = strongly agree.

_____ 1. Everyone within the organization can clearly articulate our values and our mission is clear and inspirational.

_____ 2. We all embody (live out) the values of the organization. Our "walk matches our talk."

_____ 3. Team members believe that what we do as a company impacts people's lives in a positive way.

_____ 4. We use tools and processes to select and hire team members who share our values.

_____ 5. Leaders seek a high level of buy-in from team members before implementing initiatives.

_____ 6. Cooperation and collaboration are actively encouraged and win-win resolutions are pursued.

_____ 7. Authority is delegated so that people can act responsibly to fulfill corporate objectives.

_____ 8. There is a high level of trust throughout the organization. People believe the best in each other, want the best for each other and expect the best from each other.

_____ 9. Expectations are made clear and people are held accountable for the work that they produce.

_____ 10. The organization invests heavily in developing team members and learning is an important objective in our day-to-day work.

_____ Total of scores

Rating:

90+   The culture of the organization is healthy and could be described as Remarkable!

80-90   Although this is a fairly good score, there is room for improvement. Intentional work could produce exponential returns.

70-80   An average score; lackluster performance and low engagement prevail.

<70   Unhealthy symptoms exist within the organization, greatly inhibiting performance.

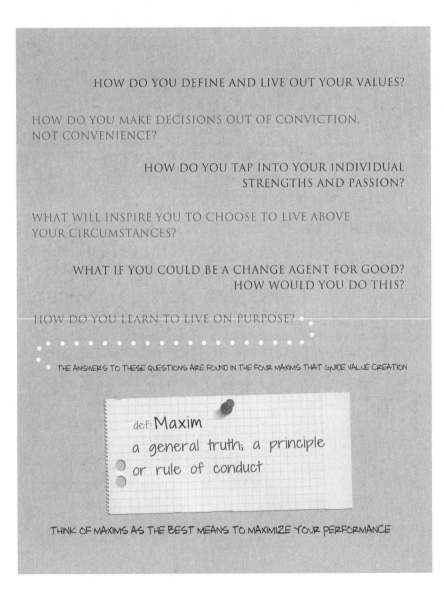

HOW DO YOU DEFINE AND LIVE OUT YOUR VALUES?

HOW DO YOU MAKE DECISIONS OUT OF CONVICTION, NOT CONVENIENCE?

HOW DO YOU TAP INTO YOUR INDIVIDUAL STRENGTHS AND PASSION?

WHAT WILL INSPIRE YOU TO CHOOSE TO LIVE ABOVE YOUR CIRCUMSTANCES?

WHAT IF YOU COULD BE A CHANGE AGENT FOR GOOD? HOW WOULD YOU DO THIS?

HOW DO YOU LEARN TO LIVE ON PURPOSE?

THE ANSWERS TO THESE QUESTIONS ARE FOUND IN THE FOUR MAXIMS THAT GUIDE VALUE CREATION

def: Maxim
a general truth; a principle or rule of conduct

THINK OF MAXIMS AS THE BEST MEANS TO MAXIMIZE YOUR PERFORMANCE

FOUR MAXIMS OF VALUE CREATION

MAXIM OF CREATIVITY
WE ARE DESIGNED TO CREATE VALUE IN LIFE

MAXIM OF POSITIVITY
AUTHENTIC POSITIVITY IS THE BY-PRODUCT OF
CREATING TRUE VALUE

MAXIM OF SUSTAINABILITY
TO CONTINUOUSLY CREATE VALUE, LEVERAGE YOUR
PASSION AND STRENGTHS TO SOLVE PROBLEMS

MAXIM OF RESPONSIBILITY
OWNERSHIP EMPOWERS PEOPLE TO TAKE
RESPONSIBILITY FOR CREATING VALUE

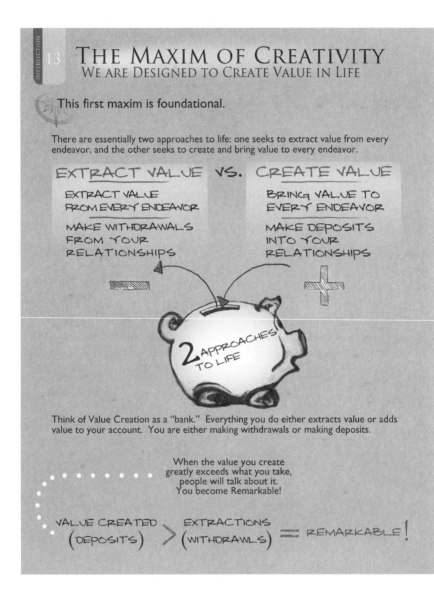

THE MAXIM OF CREATIVITY
WE ARE DESIGNED TO CREATE VALUE IN LIFE

This first maxim is foundational.

There are essentially two approaches to life: one seeks to extract value from every endeavor, and the other seeks to create and bring value to every endeavor.

EXTRACT VALUE VS. CREATE VALUE

EXTRACT VALUE
FROM EVERY ENDEAVOR

BRING VALUE TO
EVERY ENDEAVOR

MAKE WITHDRAWALS
FROM YOUR
RELATIONSHIPS

MAKE DEPOSITS
INTO YOUR
RELATIONSHIPS

2 APPROACHES TO LIFE

Think of Value Creation as a "bank." Everything you do either extracts value or adds value to your account. You are either making withdrawals or making deposits.

When the value you create
greatly exceeds what you take,
people will talk about it.
You become Remarkable!

VALUE CREATED   EXTRACTIONS
(DEPOSITS)   >   (WITHDRAWLS)   =   REMARKABLE!

Self-worth comes from the conviction that you are a person of great value and the confidence of knowing that you've made a significant contribution to a good cause. In other words, self-worth comes from knowing you have created value.

In every situation we have a choice to make – we can either seek to create value or seek to extract value. Fulfillment comes through creating as much value as possible.

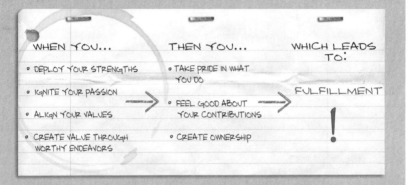

WHEN YOU...
- DEPLOY YOUR STRENGTHS
- IGNITE YOUR PASSION
- ALIGN YOUR VALUES
- CREATE VALUE THROUGH WORTHY ENDEAVORS

THEN YOU...
- TAKE PRIDE IN WHAT YOU DO
- FEEL GOOD ABOUT YOUR CONTRIBUTIONS
- CREATE OWNERSHIP

WHICH LEADS TO:

FULFILLMENT
!

GETTING TRACTION: Think of a significant relationship in your life. What's the condition of your Value Creation bank account with that person? Are you headed for relational richness or bankruptcy?

THINGS I DO THAT EXTRACT VALUE (–)

THINGS I DO THAT CREATE VALUE (+)

DESCRIBE SOME WAYS IN WHICH YOU CAN TURN SOME OF THESE WITHDRAWALS INTO DEPOSITS:

IT STARTS WITH YOU
BE THE ROLE MODEL

INTERSECTION 30

"CHANGE AROUND YOU MUST ALWAYS BEGIN WITHIN YOU."

The only way to help others learn and apply the Maxims of Value Creation is to embody them yourself.

If you are trying to transform the culture of an organization, it has to start with you.

You must choose to start the process.

You have to take the OR path.

You must assume Ownership and make Relationships your highest priority.

"BE THE CHANGE YOU WANT TO SEE IN THE WORLD."
                                                                    - GANDHI

> GETTING TRACTION: Everything begins with a choice. And, every choice is important. So, you must choose:
>
> • What kind of a leader you want be
>
> • What your vision will be for the future
>
> • Whether or not you will engage and develop others
>
> • How you will interact with others
>
> • How you will create a better self
>
> • Whether or not you will embrace problems
>
> • Whether you will create value or extract value
>
> No one else can make these decisions for you. However, if you decide to create value, you may inspire a lot of people to do the same!

"If your actions inspire others to dream more, learn more, do more and become more, you are a leader."
                                        — John Quincy Adams

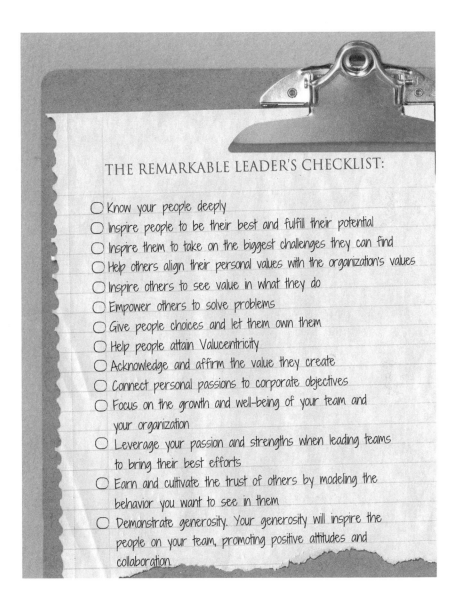

THE REMARKABLE LEADER'S CHECKLIST:

○ Know your people deeply
○ Inspire people to be their best and fulfill their potential
○ Inspire them to take on the biggest challenges they can find
○ Help others align their personal values with the organization's values
○ Inspire others to see value in what they do
○ Empower others to solve problems
○ Give people choices and let them own them
○ Help people attain Valucentricity
○ Acknowledge and affirm the value they create
○ Connect personal passions to corporate objectives
○ Focus on the growth and well-being of your team and your organization
○ Leverage your passion and strengths when leading teams to bring their best efforts
○ Earn and cultivate the trust of others by modeling the behavior you want to see in them
○ Demonstrate generosity. Your generosity will inspire the people on your team, promoting positive attitudes and collaboration.

CREATE A MOVEMENT OF GOOD

R! To change the world...
Do for ONE what you wish you could do for EVERYONE, and you will change the world for SOMEONE.

What is something you can do to make someone's story better?

INSPIRE HOPE

⚙ SEIZE THE OPPORTUNITY
⚙ GATHER THE RESOURCES
⚙ LEAD BY EXAMPLE

For resources, go to **www.RemarkableMovement.com**
and **www.CreateRemarkable.com**

Formula for Remarkable Results

Remember our premise?

REMARKABLE PEOPLE
+ REMARKABLE CULTURE
_____
REMARKABLE RESULTS

If you get this part right, everything else will be easier.

Get this wrong, and everything else will be difficult.

If you get the people part right, the right people will create the right culture.

Wherever people gather, there will be a culture.

That culture will either be by default or by design.

Craft your culture with intentionality.

When the culture is right, you will make everyone's story better. And, they will have an irrepressible desire to talk about you.

Then, you truly have become REMARKABLE.

We encourage you to begin a revolution that will infuse new life and energy into your organization and help people find significance and fulfillment in their work. We encourage you to Create Remarkable.

Life is either limited or enhanced by your choices. Leadership is about influencing people to make conspicuously unusual choices that bring health and happiness to life and work. The choices you make will eventually make you. We challenge you to choose to be Remarkable!

Appendix B

Glossary of Terms

abundance mentality—the belief that collaborating to create value can produce an abundance of resources that may be shared by those who were involved in the creative process.

axiology—the study of values, value constructs, and value creation and their subsequent impact on a person's thoughts, beliefs, decision-making processes, and performance.

clutch situation—any situation that requires two or more parties to work together, providing an opportunity for the engagement of two or more components to create progress.

Cultural Transformation Formula—Value Alignment → Thinking → Behaviors = Results (VA → T → B = R).

culture—the collective expression of the values, beliefs, and behaviors that individuals bring to an organization.

Effective Execution Formula

Quality idea (Qi) x Adoption (A) = Execution (E)

ER Factor—competing *against* others and positioning self over others—the opposite of humility. ER stands for two components that are always prominent in value extraction: ego and rivalry.

living on purpose—values-based, intentional living. Living on purpose means you live purposefully, with purpose, and for a purpose.

OR Factor (ownership and relationship)—*ownership* means that an individual assumes responsibility for their decisions and actions, while *relationship* implies an individual's desire to stay engaged with others. An emphasis on OR leads to a strong decision-making capability. OR is the only path to empowerment.

Remarkable!—notably or conspicuously unusual; extraordinary; worthy of notice or attention.

scarcity mentality—the belief that there are only limited resources in the world and that in order to survive one must deprive someone else of those resources; this perspective on life causes people to compete to extract value in each situation to ensure survival.

superior—higher in station, rank, degree, or importance; above average in excellence, merit, or intelligence; of higher grade or quality.

valucentricity—the energy and momentum that is produced when values are properly identified and aligned; producing a unified and energized work force.

Value Creation Equation—$VC = \frac{we}{me} \times OR$

Value Extraction Equation—$VE = \frac{I}{us} \times ER$

value grade—the value a person creates for and brings to an organization or endeavor, as opposed to pay grade, which speaks to the value someone extracts from the organization. When your value grade exceeds your pay grade, you become invaluable—if not indispensable—to the organization.

Sources

Arbinger Institute. *Leadership and Self-Deception.* San Francisco: Berrett-Koehler Publishers, 2010.

Buckingham, Marcus, and Donald O. Clifton. *Now, Discover Your Strengths.* New York: Free Press, 2001.

Byrum, C. Stephen. *From the Neck Up: The Recovery and Sustaining of the Human Element in Modern Organizations.* Littleton, MA: Tapestry Press, Ltd, 2006.

Byrum, C. Stephen, and Leland Kaiser. *Spirit for Greatness: Spiritual Dimensions of Organizations and Their Leadership.* Littleton, MA: Tapestry Press, Ltd, 2004.

Cathy, S. Truett. *It's Easier to Succeed than to Fail.* Nashville: Thomas Nelson, 1989.

Collins, Jim. *Good to Great.* New York: HarperCollins, 2001.

Covey, Stephen M. R. *The Speed of Trust.* New York: Free Press, 2008.

DeLong, Thomas J., and Sara DeLong. "Managing Yourself: The Paradox of Excellence." *Harvard Business Review* (June 8, 2011): 7–20.

Frankl, Viktor. *Man's Search for Meaning.* Boston: Beacon Press, 2006.

————. *Man's Search for Ultimate Meaning*. New York: Basic Books, 2000.

Hartman, Robert S. *The Structure of Value*. Carbondale, IL: Southern Illinois University Press, 1969.

Herrmann, Robert L. *Sir John Templeton: Supporting Scientific Research for Spiritual Discoveries*. Philadelphia: Templeton Press, 2004.

Milne, A. A. *The Complete Tales of Winnie-the-Pooh*. Boston: Dutton Juvenile, 1996.

Pomeroy, Leon. *The New Science of Axiological Psychology*. New York: Rodopi, 2005.

Sanders, Tim. *Love Is the Killer App*. New York: Three Rivers Press, 2002.

Seligman, Martin E. P. *Learned Optimism*. New York: Vantage Books, 2006.

Stanley, Andy. *The Principle of the Path*. Nashville: Thomas Nelson, 2011.

Acknowledgments

Acknowledgment seems like such a feeble way to express the immense gratitude we hold for those who have supported us in this project. Any success this book may experience will be due to our "tribe" of friends who have served as mentors, cheerleaders, and fans. It would be impossible to mention them all, but we would be remiss in not thanking a few. So it is with deep gratitude and humility that we would like to express our appreciation to the following folks for their contributions:

LuAnne and Lynn, our wives, for giving us more "hall passes" than we deserve and more than we should have used. Without your support and encouragement none of this would have been possible.

Chris Ferebee for championing this project. Thanks for your friendship, support, and encouragement. You are far more than our agent, you are our partner, confidant, and friend.

Chad Allen, Mark Rice, and the entire Baker Publishing Group team for believing in both the message and the messengers. We are humbled and grateful for the passion and tireless effort you've expended and for helping us broadcast the principles of value creation to a larger audience. You truly exemplify the principles espoused.

S. Truett Cathy and the entire Cathy family. Because of your faithfulness to these principles, Chick-fil-A has a corporate culture that has inspired many.

Kay Acton, Anne Alexander, and Carolyn Zauche. Without your editorial prowess, this project would have been replete with split infinitives, misspelled words, and misplaced commas. Thanks for your eagle eyes and mastery of the English language. And especially to Michelle Rapkin, whose vast experience and artful wordsmithing served to bring clarity and continuity to this project. It was a privilege and a delight to work with you.

Pat Malone for your patience, determination, and creativity in helping us bring the message to life through illustrations.

Tara Ashley for keeping us organized and making sure our busy schedules did not bottleneck the communication on this project.

Our countless friends, family members, and associates who have encouraged us to put our thoughts on paper so that others may benefit from the knowledge we've gained through our exposure to and experience with some Remarkable! companies.

About Robert S. Hartman

Robert S. Hartman, PhD, was born in Berlin, Germany, on January 27, 1910. A brilliant and energetic person, he studied at the German College of Political Science, the University of Paris (Sorbonne), the London School of Economics and Political Science, and Berlin University. By age twenty-two, he had earned his law degree and began to teach at Berlin University, while also working as an assistant district court judge.

In the early stages of his career, Hartman's life would change forever. He was witness to the emerging Hitler "system." In Hitler, he saw a man who not only was evil but also was able to organize evil. Hartman openly opposed and spoke out against Hitler and all he represented. Evading many brushes with death, Hartman faced constant danger. He was able to escape to England on a falsified passport just as the Nazis closed in on him. In England, the Walt Disney Company hired him to strategize and help the business expand into parts of Europe and South America. Hartman quickly rose through the Disney ranks, even serving as Walt Disney's personal advisor.

However, Hartman was continually haunted by the idea that Hitler had learned how to organize evil. If that was possible, was it also possible to organize goodness? He spent the rest of his life pursuing an answer to that question. The quest led him to leave Disney and begin his studies and research in the field of axiology—the science of value. His work in axiology established the relationship of values to judgment. As his work relates to business, he was referring to excellence and quality outcomes.

This thinking led him to construct the Hartman Value Profile—a tool that has been called one of the most mathematical, scientific, and logically based assessment instruments ever created. Dr. Stephen Byrum's personal work with Dr. Hartman, along with four decades of assessment interpretations and experience with the Value Profile, is the foundation for The Judgment Index™.

Hartman spent the rest of his life researching, writing, lecturing, and teaching. He earned his PhD at Northwestern University in 1946 and taught throughout the United States, Canada, Latin America, and Europe. Hartman taught at Ohio State University, Massachusetts Institute of Technology (MIT), and Yale University. Dr. Hartman was a former research professor at the University of Tennessee and the National University of Mexico. Known as the "father of modern axiology," Hartman authored more than ten books and over one hundred articles. Before his untimely death in 1973, Hartman was nominated for the Nobel Prize for his promotion of human self-understanding, the advancement of the most important human values, and the implications of his work for transforming life in the most positive ways.

For more information, visit www.hartmaninstitute.org.

About the Authors

Dr. Randy Ross is founder and CEO (Chief Enthusiasm Officer) of Remarkable!, a corporate advisory and consulting firm specializing in talent selection instruments, cultural development, and organizational health. Randy is a "craftsman of culture and a catalytic coach" whose purpose is to see others inspired and excelling in all aspects of life. Utilizing the same value-based diagnostic and developmental instruments described in this book, the *Remarkable! Philosophy* helps companies craft cultures of value creation.

Spending time in both the for-profit and not-for-profit worlds, Randy has traveled throughout the United States and the world as a speaker, consultant, and coach, building teams and developing leaders. A compelling communicator, Dr. Ross has the keen sensitivity to speak to the hearts of leaders and inspire elevated performance among teams.

For more information, or to book Randy for an engagement, please visit CreateRemarkable.com.

David Salyers has been on quite a journey. Graduating from college on a Saturday morning, he started his career with Chick-fil-A before the day was over. Currently serving as the vice president of national, regional, and local marketing for Chick-fil-A, David has spent his entire career as part of a team, committed to building the kind of company culture people talk about!

A passionate student of life and business, David has spent more than thirty years seeing the principles in this book play out corporately and in more than sixteen hundred Chick-fil-A restaurants across the country. Serving as a board member for numerous nonprofit organizations and a few for-profit start-ups has convinced him further that the principles contained within these pages are universally applicable. Having the unique opportunity to witness both great leaders and great organizations, he is energized to pass along the principles he has discovered from a personal journey, which can only be described as . . . Remarkable!

Additional Resources

Roadmap to Remarkable!

Want to translate the principles highlighted in *Remarkable!* into actionable steps? This guide will be a key resource for you and your teams.

Business as usual. It's conventional, operating within the established norms. It's predictable, delivering the expected. It's comfortable, maintaining the status quo. It's . . . safe. There are millions of organizations doing business as usual. But business as usual will never be Remarkable!

Remarkable means notably or conspicuously unusual, extraordinary, worthy of notice or attention. The ideas explored in this book have come from a lifetime of observing extraordinary people and organizations as they live out their conspicuously unusual ideas, producing uncommon results. The effect is that those who work for and those who benefit from these people and organizations find themselves with an irrepressible desire to "remark about them." What is it that these folks know that others seemingly do not? How does their view of the world lead them to think and behave differently than others? When faced with the same opportunities and challenges, how are their choices different? And why are they different?

In this guide, the principles taught in *Remarkable!* are easily explained and practically applied to transform team members into change agents who create movements of good.

Order copies at RoadmapToRemarkable.com.

Remarkable! Coin

There are riches that money can't buy. That's why we made this coin.

It's part of a movement. A movement to create a kinder and more encouraging culture, one person and one story at a time. It's easy to miss opportunities to stop and thank others for the ways in which they enrich our lives. This movement recognizes those around us who are worth celebrating. The kind ones. The generous ones. The caring ones. The ones we call Remarkable!

We live under an illusion that the size of our bank accounts determines the richness of our lives. We are drawn to opportunities to *get rich*, while missing the opportunities to *be rich* in good deeds. Most coins are designed to be deposited into a bank account, to pay for our needs, or to build wealth. The Remarkable! Coin works differently.

The coin was created to deposit into the lives of others. To help you see the good and to affirm and honor the good in others. You may give it to a stranger or to someone you know very well. Either way, you will be amazed at how taking the time to recognize and appreciate others will enrich your world.

Even after you give it away, the coin will be a treasure for you to follow on a journey that's sure to be . . . Remarkable!

Get your coins at RemarkableCoin.com.

MAKE A STATEMENT WITH YOUR LIFE

REMARKABLEMOVEMENT.COM

Remarkable! Movement

It's not just an idea, it's a movement. Join the movement and be inspired weekly when you receive a video that will both encourage and challenge you to be Remarkable! Then find and affirm the Remarkable! in your world.

When you encounter something Remarkable!, you have this irrepressible desire to share it with others. Sometimes it's an act of heroism or a demonstration of compassion. It might be a business that defies convention or a group involved in social entrepreneurship. It might even be extraordinary perseverance in the face of adversity. Whatever it is, we want to find and affirm the Remarkable! We want to create value and inspire hope by challenging the world to live life and do business on purpose, for a purpose, and with purpose.

For your free weekly inspirational video, sign up at
RemarkableMovement.com.

For engagement requests, keynotes, workshops,
and advisory services, please contact us at
CreateRemarkable.com.

REMARKABLE ENGAGEMENT INDEX

Engagement is often defined as a person's emotional attachment to any endeavor. The Remarkable Engagement Index is a unique axiological instrument that measures twelve dynamic emotional drivers of performance. Based on the Hartman Values Profile, this assessment has been dubbed one of the most scientific, mathematical, and logically based assessment tools in the market today.

....

To complete the Remarkable Engagement Index:

1. Locate your access credentials on the reverse side of the dust jacket (onetime usage).

2. Go to **CreateRemarkable.com/ei** and enter your credentials to take the assessment.

3. Once completed, your report will be delivered to the email address you provide. Please check both your in-box and filters to make sure you receive the report.

The Engagement Report will include an explanation of the various indicators, your personal score sheet, and developmental materials to help you improve emotional balance and engagement.

Additional developmental materials are available at:
RoadmapToRemarkable.com.

For information on enterprise engagements, please contact us at:
CreateRemarkable.com.

....